Final Impressions

by

Milton Kotler

Broad Branch Books

BBB

Printed in the United States of America by Broad Branch Books.

Published November 2018

ISBN 9781729459744

:

Also

by

Milton Kotler

Neighborhood Government: The Local Foundations of Political Life

Building Neighborhood Organization

A Clear-Sighted View of China Marketing

Market Your Way to Growth

Winning Global Markets

Adapt or Perish: A Journey of Wonder and Good Cheer

Dedication

I dedicate this book to Greta Kotler, a great wife, mother and professional leader, who has sustained my joy, wellbeing, and spirit for 42 years. I have tried to do the same for her.

Preface

These are stories of real people who, with several exceptions, are unknown to the reader. Each character portrayed shared the generations and historical circumstances through which I have lived, and personally came to terms or failed to do so with the conundrums of the times. Some have been dear friends, others acquaintances, and some foes. They are intimate stories of actions with moral undertones.

These are brief stories of their life, not biographies. I treat only a crisis in their lives, a moment of tangled principle and circumstance that elucidates their destiny. Their lives are much more extensive, rich, and complex then the aperçu of moral instruction through which I choose to witness them.

I choose to write these stories because, at 83, it is time for me to collect my life of personal meaning. I share a common world with my readers, so what has meaning to me could have meaning to them. A collector has to display his collection, so I offer this to you for your delight and edification.

The reader has to know something about this collector. My life is riddled through these stories, but I am obliged to present myself to you in as brief a manner as are these tales.

I was a Jewish kid on the clock in Chicago with a large and loving extended family. I had my religious and secular training as a youngster in the Windy City and then went on to the University of Chicago for 12 years of a cherished education. From there I ventured to a public policy think tank in Washington for 14 years. I married my beloved wife, Greta, in 1976 and in raising a family of four children I was impelled to leave public life for business. My marketing firm eventually took me to China for 20 years, where I continue to lead my company in building technology parks. Because I am well known in China and not in the U.S., my autobiography is published in China, in Mandarin no less. The stories told herein travel through the episodes of my life. I hope this brief resume is a sufficient canvass for my stories, which are not about me but only happened to me.

These tales are in random order. The sequence follows the course of my affections and my own emotional resonance. This should be of no concern to the reader, because each story is a nugget of reflective value.

Acknowledgements

I want to thank the following people for their assistance in preparing this book.

Neal Gillen, author and patron of the Writers' Center in Bethesda, Maryland, inspired me to publish this book. A successful independent publisher, and the author of 13 books, he knows the ropes. He guided me through the entire process, editing, proofing, and production. He is a treasured friend.

Barbara Esstman, author, editor, and instructor at the Writers' Center and American University, liked these stories and encouraged me to publish this work.

Tom Wilson of Potomac, Maryland, attorney and friend at the Club Table in the University Club's Pershing Grill, gave me critical literary and legal support.

99Designs.com helped me through the cover design process. Raphael Rafido did an excellent job of cover design.

I am blessed by the kindness of prominent China artist Wei Chuyu for crafting a gratifying sketch of me for the book cover.

Sherry Kloss provided me a photo of Ben Rosen. Michael Rosen provided a photo of Lee Haupt. Diane Silverman added material on the Dionysus story. Ralph Stavins , who was delighted with this collection of stories, encouraged me to publish them. Other University Club friends like Marty Tolchin. Michael Ledeen, John Boffa, and Paul Dragoumis enjoyed the stories.

Above all, I want thank my wife Greta Kotler for her suggestions, editing, proofing and consistent support of this literary project.

Milton Kotler

November 2018

Contents

Acknowledgements ix

Dionysus: Tom Callahan 1

Generosity: Marc Raskin 5

Compounded Faith: Pastor Leopold Bernhard 12

An Elegant Mind: Hannah Arendt 20

Friendship: David T. Bazelon 28

Lust: Paul Goodman 32

Desolation: Ramparts Magazine 38

Extortion: General Saraka 42

A Gift of the Gods: Sam Rosenkrantz 45

Prometheus: Karl Hess 54

Sweet Reason: Hilda Ellison 59

Politics: Bill Clinton 63

Statesman: Senator Mark Hatfield 69

Dignity: U.S. Rep. Henry Gonzalez 74

Glory: Ivanhoe Donaldson 79

High Spirit: Barbara Raskin 86

Musical Devotion: Ben Rosen 90

Blithe Spirit: Julian Knox 95

Conviviality: Bill Hawks 99

China: Cao "Tiger" Hu 102

Common Sense: Maurice Kotler 107

Hospitality: South Haven 114

Adventure: A Jewish Tom Sawyer 119

Serenity: Lee Haupt 128

About the Author 132

Final Impressions

.

Dionysus: Tom Callahan

It is hard for collegians today to realize that there was a time in the not so distant past, only three score years, when there was not a university mate who studied business, marketing, finance, or computer science. Indeed, it was a time when you and your college friends embraced literature, poetry, philosophy, history, classical languages, and science. It was a golden age of humanistic thought, following the slaughter of WW ll and the high tide of European refugee scholarship.

I met Tom Callahan in 1957 through Diane Silverman. Diane was a beautiful friend in the political science department of the University of Chicago. She was smart, vibrant and kind with lovely legs streamlined by her spiked heel shoes. She shared an apartment with her sister Billie, which was open and inviting to all friends day and night. The two sisters were editors of the *Hyde Park Herald* and attracted to their apartment Hyde Park notables and campus scholars.

It was at Diane's home one night that I met her friend Tom Callahan. Tom was a graduate student in classical studies. He had the handsome type of an Irish face, finer lines and less scruffy, and was erudite and poetic. He had an efflorescent flair for eloquent speech and lyrical expression. He was brilliant with an infectious humor. He paid attention to everyone in the company around him. I was smitten. We had an immediate affinity because I found him wistful and he found me inquisitive and sure-footed.

Tom was poetically Irish to the core, not from Ireland, but of Irish being. As a result, he seemed foreign, though born and raised in New York, and never to my knowledge having visited Ireland. His parents were alcoholics and he was taken from his parents and raised by an aunt. He matriculated at St. Johns College in Annapolis and then went to Berkeley for classical studies. He came to the University of Chicago after a stint in the Merchant Marines to continue his classical studies in Greek and Latin.

At the University he was startlingly singular with no shadow of family and old friends. He attached himself to whomever he was with. The gals were enthralled by his good looks, flashing brain, and the fixed attention that he gave to each of them. The guys were charmed by this unusual spirit in their midst.

Tom and I spent a lot of time together at Diane's apartment with her flow of friends and their enlightened conversations. Tom's lips were always touched by wine and liquor. His vinous succor kept him going hour after hour and day after day. I was inebriated myself, but not to his degree.

He was never drunk in any slobbering sense. Wine was his tonic for imaginative speech. The one time that I saw him drunk was at a festive party. We left the party and Tom drove my car directly into a parked car. My car was totaled, and I went to the hospital with a broken leg. There was no pause in the time we spent together. In fact he cared for me and moved into the basement apartment of my building. Our bond thickened.

Tom was never sober. He only pretended to be sober on occasions that warranted this appearance. He was never morose. The more he drank, the higher his language soared. Drink formed his imagination into artful expression. After I left Chicago, Tom visited me and my then wife Janet at our apartment in Washington, DC. We spent a night of drink, talk, and slumber. The next morning Janet prepared a breakfast of orange juice, bacon and eggs. Tom set aside his citrus and requested glass of whiskey as his morning juice. It was 10 a.m. and we thereafter spent a delightful and absorbing day of conversation with no want of brilliance on his part. I celebrated the day by giving him my treasured volume of Robert Burns' poetry.

I came to the conclusion that wine was intrinsic to Tom. There was no difference between a besotted Tom and a sober Tom. He was in fact, true to his Greek studies — an acolyte of Dionysus. The only difference in his behavior was the lyrical tempo befitting changing circumstances. He was festive in a festive circumstance, lyrical in a poetical circumstance, dialectical in a philosophic circumstance, but always intoxicated with a miraculous capacity to appear sober. This incredible ability to appear sober was basic to his sustenance. He actually managed to get through law school and work on important legal projects like the estimable Jury Project of the University of Chicago Law School. He held other jobs for brief periods and executed the greatest feat of apparent sobriety by getting married and fathering a child. That vaulted feat was his final undoing.

I left Chicago in 1963 and followed his catastrophic affairs through Diane and other friends. Tom's marriage to Jean was a tragic misalliance. She was not one of the adoring gals who pined for him, but a stern gal whom he married as a crucible of stability and success. Jean eventually threw him out and severed his relationship to his son, Gaylan. Tom fell into despair and clung for dear life to Diane and her husband Lou. Kind-hearted Diane took Tom into their home and embraced him as a member of the family. Diane and Lou had three children. Tom was never again to see Gaylan, though Jean lived four blocks away. The alcoholism that separated him from his father haunted his separation from his own son.

Tom rotated in and out of hospitals as his organs began to fail when he was in his late 40s. He finally was able to launch his own apartment, but only for a short period of time. He ate his dinners with the Silverman's, as he declared to Diane that her home was "his only real home." One night he did not come for dinner. When he failed to arrive the second night a worried Diane went to his apartment. There was no answer. She prevailed on the super to open the door. There lay the half-mortal Dionysus, dead!

Tom was Dionysus, forever chaotic and unexpected, escaping human reality at all cost, and finding his only respite in the hearth of his mortal mother Semele. It is impossible to say what earthly heights Tom could have reached with his enormous talent, but for drink. His talent was essentially bibulous, fermented in the wine of the gods. It is like asking how high a three-footed goat could climb a mountain.

Generosity: Marc Raskin

Marcus Raskin, founder and leader of the Institute for Policy Studies (IPS) in Washington, D.C., died in January 2018. He was a beloved figure of the American Left. That February, nearly a thousand people attended his memorial service at the historic Synagogue at 6th and I Street. They came from all over the country and abroad to honor a man who did so much for them. The speakers hailed his kindness and generosity. Marc gave many of them a chance to do their worldly work. He built their careers in the panoply of political causes spanning disarmament, identity politics, anti-war activity, third world left-wing insurrection, and every stripe of radical action. He was acclaimed as a master fundraiser and strategist for every assault on conventional Democrat Party liberal politics. Their pulverizing and idiosyncratic success of his audience fatally eclipsed his own liberalism, fractured the Democrat Party, and set the stage for the rise

5

and dominance of the political right.

As an early friend of Marc and colleague for 14 years at IPS, I can attest to the sincerity of this veneration. There was no other figure on the American left that succored radical action like he did. The only real question is whether in fact he was too generous, to the detriment of his own liberal foundation.

Generosity is the golden mean of human sharing. Too little generosity is a vice of niggardliness or stinginess; too much generosity is a wasteful dissipation of resources and principle. If one were to search for fault in Marc, it would be the vastness of his generosity. He wanted to do well for the world and advanced many individuals who did good and notable works, as well as others who contrived spurious new social and political vales or failed to deliver real value. To sustain and foster his liberal ideals required a constant search for funding that took him in varied directions. With his declining health, he lost the stamina to guide his collective of activists. They spun off in the political atmosphere like shooting stars, gone in the blinking of an eye.

Marc's generosity required intense fundraising from deep sources of money. It is one thing to be generous with one's own money. To be generous with other people's money makes one beholden to the social views of the shifting sources of money, each source having its own views on policies of how best to pursue and accomplish social reconstruction. This resulted in conflicting views on how to best accomplish Marc's desired social ends within the limits of our political institutions and the lives of Americans.

Marc was raised in Milwaukee, Wisconsin. As an accomplished pianist, following high school, he went on to the famed Julliard School in New York City, and then to the college of the University of Chicago and to its law school. After his marriage to Barbara Bellman and a musical year in Italy, he landed in Washington, D.C., where he began a political career on the policy staff of Congressman Sidney Yates (D-IL) of Chicago. During the administration of John F. Kennedy, he joined the White House staff of Mc George Bundy, President Kennedy's national security advisor. With his friend Richard Barnet, who was with the U.S. Disarmament Administration, they planned a liberal think tank. Their vision was an independent liberal center of public policy, free of government money and thus able to speak truth to power.

Marc secured enough private funding to start IPS with a small permanent core of young political intellectuals. I was one of this group of five, which included along with Marc and Dick, Christopher Jencks, who was an editor of the *New Republic* magazine, and Arthur Waskow, who worked for Congressman Robert Kastenmeier (D-WI). We were all in our late 20s and were joined by three older visiting fellows (a term of three years): novelist Paul Goodman; David T. Bazelon, attorney and author of *The Paper Economy;* and Leo Szilard, the inventor of the nuclear chain reaction in 1933, who after collaborating on the creation of the atomic bomb in the Manhattan Project, later turned passionately to nuclear disarmament. We were ensconced in an old mansion at 19th and T Streets.

Marc was a charismatic figure who attracted a cadre of social action thinkers from the university and literary worlds. His personal magnetism drew hundreds of activists to IPS and opened a wide orbit of political action. He was short, slight and rumpled looking with an inventive mind, thick eye glasses, enormous energy, and a modest personality. Women loved his ambition and men admired his gravity. Marc had a talent for emboldening people.

Our first IPS projects were progressive. Christopher was designing an innovative public school system for the new planned town of Columbia, Maryland. Arthur and I were running a civil rights seminar, from which endeavor the Presbyterian Church of America sent me to Mississippi to plan the new Delta Ministry Project to help rural blacks. Marc and Dick ploughed new ground on détente with the Soviet Union and arms control. Goodman used his book, *Growing Up Absurd,* to inspire young people to buck convention for new paths of personal freedom. Szilard organized scientists to resist development of nuclear weapons. Arthur agitated for human rights and Bazelon critiqued American politics.

IPS was welcomed by the Kennedy-Johnson era as a liberal cohort in government and in the Congress. We were exciting to the press and to liberal-minded foundations. The climax of this first era of IPS was the Anti-Vietnam war demonstrations, in which Marc played a leadership role. He dared the law and prevailed against criminal indictment for his anti-draft mobilization work. He won in the streets, in the courts of law, and in the chambers of Congress.

Marc lent IPS as a platform and financial resource for young activists to pursue their cause of change. He had an instinct for social action, rather than for scholarship. He seemed to know which people had the stamina and talent for creative disruption and struggle and only needed a platform and salary from IPS to accomplish important public work.

I was a recipient of his generosity. He gave me the freedom to formulate and implement my ideas on neighborhood government. He gave Arthur Waskow the freedom and funding to transform his human rights agenda into the ethnic crusade of Jews for Urban Justice, which nourished Arthur's spirit to later become a Rabbi of Jewish renewal.

He funded Topper Carew as a young black architect to develop and operate the New Thing, a space for creative black culture and arts. John Wilson came to IPS as a student from Howard University and went on to become Chairman of the City Council of Washington DC. Ivanhoe Donaldson came as a Fellow from SNCC and went on to become Deputy Mayor of Washington, DC., Stokely Carmichael tested his ideas and rhetoric at IPS seminars.

Ralph Stavins became a principal agent of the disclosure of the Pentagon Papers to the New York Times. Marc welcomed a young lesbian activist, Rita Mae Brown, who went on to become a prominent novelist. Marc provided a position for libertarian Karl Hess, Barry Goldwater's speech writer, and supported his innovation of community technology. Marc sponsored Orlando Letelier as a Fellow. Orlando was the Ambassador from Chile to the United States until the coup d'état that overthrew the Salvador Allende regime. IPS became his home until he was assassinated on the streets of Washington, D.C. The list goes on and on of Marc's generous institutional and financial support of notable activists, as well as many who were just out of the box. His generosity was magnanimous.

The Vietnam War was the metamorphous of IPS. Some of our major donors were staunch liberal allies of Lyndon Johnson who supported the war. IPS was breaching the border of anti-Communist Democrat party liberalism, and entering a no-man's land just short of radicalism. I remember an evening in 1967 when we hosted Jerry Wurf of AFSME and Leonard Woodcock of the UAW to plead with them to oppose the war, to no avail.

As IPS moved against the war, the first generation of our liberal donors exited. Marc's anti-war prominence and support of Third-World liberation opened new doors of funding from wealthy families in New York and California who were far left of a liberal center.

Marc brought Saul Landau to IPS. He was a leading Cubanista figure from political circles in Berkeley, California, who was familiar with Hollywood figures that were assailed during the McCarthy period. He produced a notable documentary of Fidel Castro and visited Cuba as a friend of Castro.

Saul introduced Cora Weiss to IPS. He had dated Cora at University of Wisconsin. She was a daughter of Samuel Rubin, president of Faberge cosmetics, a brand Sam acquired from the Soviet Union with the assistance of his friend Armand Hammer, who made his fortune supplying the Bolshevik government with Western medicine. Rubin, a generous person, who enjoyed the finer things in life, including his extensive collection of Rembrandt's and the other great masters, was rough around the edges and difficult to deal with. Rubin soon enlisted friends to support IPS. His efforts provided the lion's share of IPS funding during the decade of the 1970s, resulting in Peter Weiss, Cora's husband, becoming chairman of the IPS board.

With Marc's support, Saul Landau brought in new international Fellows to IPS. IPS purchased a building in Amsterdam that was named the Transnational Institute. Marc urged me to visit it, which I did. It was a hot-bed of revolutionary-minded European, African and Latin American organizers. Its impact came home to me when the Washington Fellows were asked to describe their work to Sam Rubin. He commented on my neighborhood government presentation with a scornful remark, "Cockroach capitalism!" The other Fellows in domestic policy met a similar reproach.

The assassination of Orlando Letelier was a decisive tipping point for IPS. Marc formed a close alliance with Saul and the Rubin internationalist funders. The rationale was "Euclidian." Barnet had written a seminal book on the globalization of American corporate power — "If American corporate power is international, the resistance must be international."

The focus would soon shift from problems at home to those

abroad. Within a year of Letelier's death, the IPS board decided to reduce the salaries of all Fellows by 50 percent, requiring each of us to raise the other half. By this time, the policy staff had grown to about 50 people. Most of us were involved in domestic public policy and had no ability to independently raise private money to fund our respective activities. Since the international contingent retained full board funding, we organized an AFL/CIO union to oppose management. Marc urged me to remain with management, but I saw no future for my domestic neighborhood organizing work at IPS. Marc had earlier asked me several times to organize a neighborhood delegation to go the Cuba, which I declined to do.

I joined the union out of sympathy for the liberal domestic program. The union failed, and its members started their own collective with a cash settlement from IPS. I had my own foundation funding for neighborhood government work, which I was able to take with me. I departed with my funding and set up the headquarters of the National Association of Neighborhoods (NAN). I said farewell to IPS.

In the ensuing years of my business life, which began in 1980, I would occasionally have lunch dates with Marc. "What is going on in the business world?" he would quizzically ask. "What is going on in the public policy world?" I would winsomely answer. We spoke past each other.

Marc started an impressive liberal intellectual center of public policy. His generosity and the generosity of liberal funders brought a bevy of good thinkers to IPS, some of whom left a legacy of legislation and thought. Marc's refusal to engage in the structure of the Democrat Party turned off some liberal contributions. The Vietnam War and the resulting anti-war activism took him and many progressive thinking Americans in a different direction during the Nixon years.

It is my belief that this tact was damaging to the Democrat Party. Had he engaged it at this critical juncture, he could have positively shaped it and in doing so perpetuated workable liberalism. Instead, he moved away from it, spawning views too far from the moderately-liberal party stalwarts. This deconstruct, far from the center, isolated him from having a more influential effect on public policy. There is no question that his brilliance and persuasive ability would have accomplished that end. Still, Marc is a shining example of dedication to one's ideals. In the minds of many, including mine, he is a saint.

Compounded Faith:

Pastor Leopold Bernhard

"Hybrids are sometimes stronger than either parent variety, a phenomenon called heterosis, hybrid vigour, or heterozygote advantage." David Stokes, *"Evaluating the Utility of Arabidopsis Thaliana as a Model for Understanding Heterosis in Hybrid Crops." Euphytica 156,* Issue 1-2 (July 2007) 151-71.

"Milton, please take these two boxes of Leopold's letters and hide them. I do not want them to go to the archives." I did as Thelma entreated. The boxes are still hidden in my home 32 years later. Please be patient, dear reader; I will tell you what these boxes contain as my story unfolds.

Leopold Bernhard was my moral and political mentor during three decades of the 1960s to the 1980s of my neighborhood government work at the Institute for Policy Studies (IPS) and the

National Association of Neighborhoods (NAN). He was my comrade in arms since our first neighborhood government project was initiated in his parish church in Columbus, Ohio, in 1965.

Leopold was Pastor of the First English Lutheran Church in Columbus when we met in 1964 at the Urban Training Center for Christian Missions. We engaged very easily and spoke a good deal. He was a tall and handsome gentleman in his early fifties. I was 30 at the time. Leopold came from an aristocratic family in Lubeck. Germany. His grandfather invented and manufactured corrugated steel production and added great wealth to a long lineage of Hanseatic nobility. His mother was the protagonist in Thomas Mann's novel *Buddenbrooks*. He grew up in a magisterial estate with books and music, and had a special taste for fine Gewürztraminer wine. When we met his refined face and powerful forehead was crowned with a truss of receding hair. His chin was strong and his mouth was wide and gentle. He had a remarkably intelligent and determined face.

Leopold fled Germany in 1937. He went to Switzerland for his theological degree. Upon his return to Nazi Germany he was inducted into the army and refused to serve. His family whisked him out of the country with 10 dollars in his pocket and gold cufflinks. He landed in New York and managed to get an assignment to a church in Gary, Indiana, through the Lutheran Church of America (LCA). In 1939, he investigated a ruckus of laughter from his parish hall in Gary and found his congregants drinking and hailing a film of the Nazi bombardment of Poland. He stopped the show and reproached his flock of German-American parishioners for their barbarous behavior. He left with their collection box for the Nazis. The next day a trusted congregant warmed him of physical danger and urged him leave town. Death threats followed and Leopold, upon advice from the FBI, left town with his wife Thelma and her daughter Thelma, Jr. The LCA found him another parish in rural New Jersey.

In 1938, his parents and sister visited from Germany. He urged them to remain in the U.S., but they declined. His family had prominent positions in industrial, financial, and academic life. They declined and were all tragically killed in the Dresden fire-bombing of 1945.

Leopold wrote a book with Kresman Taylor called *Until that Day*, describing the Nazi takeover of the Lutheran Church in Germany. He used a pseudonym to hide his identity because of his family in Germany. It was a best seller and has been recently republished in Germany. He died in 1984.

I met Leopold at the Urban Training Center for Christian Missions in 1964 where he was a visiting pastor. Rev. James Morton invited me to Chicago to discuss my neighborhood organizing work and neighborhood government theory to his collaborative of socially active Protestant ministers. I had been doing community organizing in the Woodlawn area of Chicago's South Side during my student days at the University of Chicago, and I had traveled to Mississippi for the Delta Ministry project. Morton had read my papers on community organizing and was intrigued by the novelty of my thought. I had worked with Saul Alinsky, who was the radical rage at the time, and, like a good Protestant, Morton was curious about my deviation from the Alinsky canon, which was top down leadership. I advocated bottom up leadership and broke with Alinsky in 1961.

Leopold was an illustrious member of the LCA clergy. He was pastor of the First English Lutheran Church in Columbus, Ohio, which was an old and well-heeled white church in a neighborhood that had become black. He was searching for a positive and theologically sound solution to his parish conundrum. What could a white church do in a black neighborhood? Of all the visiting ministers, he most actively engaged my thought. He invited me to come to Columbus to see his church and neighborhood to see what we could do.

I went to Columbus and spent the next four years working with Leopold to build the neighborhood government of the East Central Citizens Association (ECCO). The essential principle of neighborhood government was to organize neighborhood communities to directly govern local public assets, like schools, community centers, libraries and other public centers of important value to the community. Our model of governance was direct-assembly government, based on the American heritage of town-meeting government and the Jeffersonian vision of the Ward Republic. Our evidence of this community capability for governance was the historic fact that urban neighborhoods were municipal towns before their externally contrived annexation by powerful central towns. Their local liberty was seized.

Chicago annexed scores of municipalities, which are now called the "neighborhoods" of Chicago, for the political and economic interests of "downtown." The same thing happened in Pittsburgh, New York, Philadelphia, Boston and cities across America. This was for political and economic aggrandizement, not purported efficiency.

The pragmatic premise of our position is that small communities are capable of self-government because they had historically done so. The moral premise is that human lives are fulfilled by their direct deliberative responsibility for the affairs of their local community.

In the case of ECCO, the community was predominantly Afro-American and working class. The First English Lutheran church had a community center, which we planned to transfer as a physical asset to ECCO once its neighborhood government structure was in place and the community elected to receive and operate the Center as its own public asset.

With funding support from the Federal Government, it took three years of hard work of many neighborhood leaders to achieve this objective. Leopold and I bonded by our guidance of this goal. We were colleagues in a quest for human responsibility, achieving our objective when, in 1968, the church formally transferred the center's deed to ECCO in an exalting ceremony of liberty.

Leopold and I went on to organize neighborhood governments in many cities as we formed a national leadership federation called the Alliance of Neighborhood Government (ANG), which thereafter became the National Association of Neighborhoods (NAN), an organization that exists to this day. Greta Kotler, ne Smith, was my principal Washington colleague.

As I noted earlier Leopold was older and of a different background when we began our collaboration. I was a political scientist at IPS and free to pursue my activity as I wished through the generosity of Marc Raskin. I had political support in the Johnson administration and Congress. Though I could not personally receive federal money, I raised a lot of government grants and contract money for community organizations to directly run federal government and foundation-funded programs in their own

15

neighborhoods.

While my motivation was philosophical, Leopold was moved by religious conviction. The roots of his passion for political freedom lay in his biblical faith and in his own personal life. Leopold never preached to me, but I did read many sermons he composed for his church in Columbus. In the first instance, he was a scholar. His sermons were always rooted in biblical text. He would select text according to the liturgical schedule of readings, and interpret text to advance his parishioners' understanding and judgment of the paramount social or political issues of the day. He also guided their thought and action on the perennial cycle of family and personal issues. His key was biblical insight. He led his congregants to think biblically, not as fundamentalists but as pragmatic citizens.

His sermons were rich in Old Testament scripture. He confessed to me his adoration of the historical nature of Judaism. He had a unique and trenchant way of illuminating political issues from a biblical perspective. His sermons were compelling because of their biblical rigor and practical salience.

In 1968, Leopold left Columbus for a parish in Rochester, New York. In short order he came to Washington to assume a pastorate in public affairs at the Lutheran Church of the Reformation on Capitol Hill. This involved counseling members of Congress and staff and convening monthly discussions on political affairs for the congregation. He asked me to join the board of the Lutheran Public Affairs Council, so I became a Jewish official in the LCA.

With Leopold in Washington we continued to work together. I was welcomed to his home by his wife, Thelma, whom I loved dearly. Leopold and I established the Institute for Neighborhood Government at IPS with independent private money, which examined theoretical and historical issues of democratic local self-governance. We also conducted a seminar on religion and politics with leading theologians. My IPS colleagues were skeptical about this endeavor, but they were informed of a sector of political discourse that they had never considered. This was years before the strong emergence of evangelical Christianity in American politics.

Leopold married Greta and me in a dual Christian and Jewish exchange of vows. My children were converted to Judaism, while

Greta remained a Presbyterian. Leopold and Thelma's daughter Thelma, Jr., and her family, and our families merged in a trusted bond of friendship that lasted to his death in 1986.

Leopold confided to me that his paternal grandfather, the inventor of corrugated steel, was Jewish and that he had always been fascinated by this heritage. No one in the church knew of this patrimony. Thelma had always felt that this knowledge would compromise his esteemed reputation in the national Church and in his current parish, as well as endanger his pension.

As the closest of friends, I marveled at Leopold's scholarship and social and human insight. He was a buoyant spirit and a great comfort to people. He loved me as the son he never had, and he admired my innovative mind. He adored my wife and children, and he and Thelma celebrated holidays along with us. He was a guest at our farm in Vermont and at Greta's summer cottage on Chesapeake Bay. We went boating together, always talking about the world.

Now I return to the boxes that Thelma urged me to secrete. Leopold had a history of kidney cancer. He reached a point that required dialysis treatment. He did this for several years until the treatment lost its efficacy. He would fall out of bed and frequently collapse. Leopold was six foot tall, and he dreaded the trauma of Thelma, who was a small woman, trying to get him up from the floor. He could not bear her hardship and decided to end his life so she might live in peace. He terminated his dialysis which meant certain death in two weeks. He moved to the hospital for hospice care. I visited every day for conversation. Thelma was with him, as well as the music of Bach Masses and cantatas, which he adored. His church choir came to the hospital to sing to him. He had a blessed smile on his face as he approached death. He died in peace.

Thelma and Arnold Keller, his colleague and principal pastor of his church, asked me to deliver the eulogy at his funeral mass. I wrote a sublime encomium delivered with tears of tribute. Arnold asked me to continue on the Public Affairs Council. At a dinner council meeting a church member commented to me about my close relationship with Leopold and how unusual it was that he emphasized Old Testament scripture in his sermons. She was on to something! Her suspicion rested at on the fact that many German Jews had converted to the Lutheran faith and even served in the church. I said nothing.

Thelma asked me to be executor of Leopold's vast library and personal papers. I sold the books and invited our friend Robert Jenson, then at Gettysburg Lutheran Seminary, to help sort his papers for archival deposit at his seminary. I said nothing to Bob about the two boxes concealed in my home.

The boxed contained urgent and desperate letters from Leopold to Lutheran church bodies and seminaries in America, Australia, Canada, U.K. and elsewhere trying to find a position away from Nazi Germany. There were official "Heil Hitler" letters declaring that as a Michling (part Jew, part Aryan) he could not serve in any church position in Germany. There were regretful letters from friendly theologians and pastors who promised to help him find a position abroad. There were family letters that shared his shock and wished him well. There were foreign letters that either said there were no available positions or proposed to examine the possibilities of an opening. Since the letters numbered in the hundreds, I asked a German violin friend of mind to help me decipher some of the Gothic *Gebrochene Schrift*, (Broken Script) that I could not read, except for the "Heil Hitler" salutations.

Years later in my 70s after Thelma's death, I telephoned her daughter, Thelma Jr., and asked her to receive her father's letters. They would perish with my passing, and she had children who would have an interest in their grandfather's life. I told her that I was true to my pledge to her mother never to publicly reveal their contents. "The ball is in you court," I implored. "Mr. Kotler, do not send the boxes to me, I will not accept them." I recoiled, "Thelma, he was your father. How can you decline?" She responded that she knew what the letters were about and wanted nothing to do with it. Thelma, Jr. refused responsibility for reasons of shame. She was Leopold's adopted daughter from her mother' s first marriage, so there was no blood shame, only a smudge of medieval anti-Semitism that still coursed through her veins. "So be it," I concluded. The letters are still with me somewhere in my old house. My son Jonathan, who reads German, may read these letters someday. Leopold was his god-father.

Leopold was never ashamed of his Jewish heritage. He was privately proud. How could he despise a grandfather who invented corrugated steel and augmented the prominence of his family? Old Bernhard married into aristocracy. There was a personal reality that underscored Leopold's Old Testament sermon allusions. That was the devotion of a Michling to Judaism, not the shame of a Michling. The Michling found a kindred spirit in a whole Jew, and we were blessed with a profound friendship.

An Elegant Mind: Hannah Arendt

"Who somebody is or was we can only know by knowing the story of which he is himself the hero...his biography, as it were; everything else we know of him, including the works he may have produced and left behind, tells us only what he is or was." Hannah Arendt, *The Human Condition*, p.186.

Hannah Arendt was one of the most preeminent political philosophers of the 20th century. Her thought is propounded in the *Origins of Totalitarianism, The Human Condition, On Revolution, Eichmann in Jerusalem, On Violence, Between Past and Future,* and other brilliant and intellectually gripping works. I was blessed to know her as a friend and offer this story only to provide a glimpse into her "who-ness." While she never wrote her own story, her excellent biographer, Elisabeth Young-Bruehl, who wrote *For Love of the World*, welcomed these anecdotes.

   Hannah was in her 60s when she came to the Institute for Policy Studies (IPS) in the 1960s. She was a beautiful woman, in the sense of rare beauty possessed by the penetrating intellect of a woman of the world. Her classical European schooling was gently etched in her kind face. Her eyes were attentive but soft. Her lips were wide and endearing. Her nose was sculpted to pick up the moral scent of her surroundings. Her slim legs were seductive, as she carried her age with aplomb. She smoked constantly, and her vapor enveloped her surrounding admirers. The tone of her voice was gracious and probing. She preferred to learn rather than to teach. What an unusual woman! There was an equal weight of intelligence and sensuality in her mind. In short, she was an irresistible intellectual woman at a time when few women were not intellectually renowned.

Hannah Arendt was a periodic Visiting Fellow at IPS during my years as a Resident Fellow. Before I came to Washington, I attended her lectures on *The Human Condition* and *On Revolution* at the University of Chicago in 1958 and 1962. She joined the faculty of the Committee on Social Thought in 1963 after I had left the university. She came to IPS for two week periods for several years during the Vietnam War and conducted seminars and conversational circles.

My first meeting with her was the occasion of her first IPS visit in 1967. She was invited to participate in a morning seminar on civil rights. I recall that Clyde Ferguson, the black Dean of the Howard University Law School impressed her a great deal. He had a probing intelligence and she was not used to black intellectuals. Among my colleagues mention earlier, Barnet, as usual, said nothing during the seminar. Bazelon was voluble as usual; Goodman, thoughtful; Raskin, strategic; Waskow, irascible; Jencks, circumspect; and I, reverent. We discussed the paramount issues of civil rights and decolonization in Africa.

After the seminar Marc, Richard, Christopher, James R. Newman, Thurmond Arnold, and I took Hannah to lunch at the Cosmos Club. We wanted to honor her presence in Washington with lunch at this prestigious institution. There was one problem, a paradox that none of us anticipated. We were embarrassed by an archaic rule. A woman could not enter the front door of this men's Club or eat in the main dining hall. Consequently, led by our host Newman, we had to go around to the rear of the Club and enter a side door to the empty breakfast room where the Club staff set up a special table for seven of us. We ate in seclusion, while male members and their guests dined in the splendid dining hall. Arendt was amused by this "segregation." After her life in Germany of Nazi bigotry and repeated escape from death, this separation of the sexes was a pittance of stupidity that she managed with wit, charm, and driving intelligence during our "special" luncheon.

One of her visits followed the publication in 1970 of Arthur Waskow's, *Freedom Haggadah* (The Haggadah is the book that is used during the Seder on Passover eve on the first two evenings of Passover). Arthur had included hip "freedom fighters" in his Haggadah — Huey Newton, Castro, Bobby Seale, Che Guevara, etc. … and Hannah Arendt. One evening at an Institute party during her visit, she pulled me aside and implored me to arrange a private meeting with Arthur to discuss the inclusion of her name in his Haggadah. She was horrified to come across this, which someone had brought it to her attention.

I called Arthur and the three of us met behind closed doors. "Arthur," she begged, "Why did you do this? What is my name doing here? How can you create such an assemblage of persons in a Haggadah? What does this have to do with the Passover?" He tried to explain. She looked at him as if he were a madman. His explanation made no sense to her. She was gracious, but begged him, "Take my name out of this book, I beg you." Arthur was saddened by her request.

I visited Hannah on several occasions at her 370 Riverside Drive apartment in New York City. She was bemused that the door man allowed me to go directly to her apartment. "How did they let you pass? They always stop Auden when he comes to visit. He is so disheveled." Her apartment was cascaded with books and she had her own study off the living room. We settled in the living room for our talk. Hannah asked me why I was not smoking. I had been a heavy smoker until 1972, when I was forced by medical circumstance to give up the pleasure. I told her of the circumstance. After a meeting in my office at 5 p.m., having already smoked several packs of cigarettes that day, I had an unusual experience of not being able to swallow. I could not contract my throat and swallow. I began to gag. I could not take in oxygen or expel carbon dioxide. I was suffocating.

I panicked and asked Greta, who was my colleague on neighborhood government at the time, to get me a taxi to the hospital. We shortly arrived at the George Washington University Hospital emergency room, where I continued to gag but was apparently breathing without realizing it.

The attending physician examined me and assured me that I would not die. My trachea was inflamed and narrowed. Some bronchial phlegm got stuck in the narrow passage. An expiration of that phlegm would solve the problem. He proceeded to harness my chest with his arms and with one blow expelled the substance.
He told me that I should not be alarmed. If this should happen again, I would fall unconscious and my autonomic nerve system would take over and secure my breathing function. Someone would eventually come by and call an ambulance. I would be treated in the hospital and be back to normal.

The prospect of someone coming along on the streets of Washington, D.C., to call an ambulance was horrendously implausible. I asked him for a cure. No cure! My trachea was inflamed by my smoking, "Have no fear; you won't die," he said. The doctor never once suggested that I give up smoking. Then and there, I took my half pack of Kent cigarettes from my pocket and threw it in the waste bin. That was 1972, and I have never smoked cigarettes again, only cigars after 1988

This was the story that I told Hannah to explain my I wasn't smoking cigarettes. Her reply was that this circumstance had happened to her several times. She had been resuscitated on each occasion. I asked her why she had not given up smoking. She replied, "For no reason?"

I visited her after the publication of my book, *Neighborhood Government*, which she praised. On that occasion, Hannah presented me with an elegant plate of hors d' oeuvres with caviar and truffles. She drank Campari, I drank Scotch. I believe she switched to bourbon as the talk went on. After a couple of hours of drinking, smoking and talking about politics, she declined my request to extend her visits to IPS, but she agreed to continue annual visits. When we went out to dinner, Hannah flagged a taxi with her formal white glove.

I never met Hannah's husband, Heinrich Blucher. He remained in his back study without ever coming to the living room to meet his wife's guest. He was a professor of German literature at Bard College. After he died in 1970 he was buried at Bard.

Arendt was interested in my work on neighborhood government and community organization for local self-government. She wrote a compelling testimonial for *Neighborhood Government*. We had discussed neighborhood organization on many occasions when she visited IPS. My work was influenced by her writings on the Greek Polis, the French Commune, workers' councils, and the Jeffersonian Ward Republic. She broached a personal subject.

"Milton, the landlord across the street is doing a terrible thing," she said, pointing to a formerly well-turned, but now decrepit high-rise residential building across the street. "He is forcing the rent-control tenants out by filling the building with Puerto Ricans who are destroying the building. The landlord is not repairing anything." I replied that the old tenants should remain and organize the building with the new Puerto Rican tenants. "Organize them!" she replied. "Why not?" I asked. She replied with a modicum of hesitation, "They are illiterate, and driven by necessity. They cannot be free to act. You cannot organize them. The old tenants will be driven out until only the Puerto Ricans will remain." I responded, "The Puerto Ricans can organize for their own wellbeing." She replied that they are too poor to organize. "You cannot organize them. They will be driven out, too."

I was struck by her adherence to the principles of freedom that she laid out in the *Human Condition*. The poor, she claimed, do not politically act. Political action requires a secure economic foundation. In the streets of New York she was consistent. This very point puzzled me about her endorsement of my book. My book was about the neighborhood government of a low-income black community.

She thought they were too poor to act politically. I rejoined that they worked for a living, had families and churches, and owned or rented their modest homes for years. It was this black working class base that made ECCO work. She could not imagine the Puerto Ricans as working people. "They are on welfare," she declared. I concurred that welfare was a threat to their capacity for freedom.

On another visit, I mentioned that I had a UK edition of her book *Rahel Varnhagen: The Life of a Jewess*. I found this 1957 edition published by the Leo Baeck Institute in London in Rosenblum's Jewish bookstore on Lawrence Avenue in Chicago. At that time, it had not been published in the U.S. My discovery of this rare work, considering Arendt's intellectual esteem, surprised me.

"Why has it not been published in the U.S.?"

She replied, "It is not much of a work, but I will tell you a story. This was a dissertation I had written in Germany when I was a student. In the early 1930s, I gave this manuscript to Gershom Scholem for possible publication, but he returned it as 'unfit.' I thought nothing of the matter for years after. At the end of the war, I received a call from Scholem. He was at the Leo Baeck Institute in London and asked me, 'Hannah, you have an essay on a German Jewess, am I correct?' 'You are correct,' I replied, 'Rahel Varnhagen. 'You saw the manuscript years ago and didn't think much of it.' He responded, 'But now we need it. We must publish it. May we?' 'Why now?' she asked. 'To prove we were there.'" Such a story! Arendt's lips were pursed and desolate as I left her apartment.

After the death of her husband, Hannah visited IPS. This visit followed the publication of her book, *On Violence*. Marc, Dick and I decided to invite her to become a Resident Fellow. We agreed that I would extend the invitation. Hannah and I were walking on Connecticut Avenue at R Street when I raised the issue of our desire to have her in permanent residence. This was in 1972. She firmly declined, saying that she was too old for politics. Her full attention was now devoted to her next book, *The Life of the Mind*. Politics was a young parson's activity and middle-aged person's concern. She had been a spectator for the past decades, but now she was too old even for that. She was ready *for vita compliva;* how true to her categories of thought. She had lived her life, she explained. Now, as an old person, she wanted not to act or watch, but to think – *The Life of the Mind.* Washington was a political city, not a place for thought. She thanked us "for so kindly wishing to take in an old lady," but declined the offer.

I introduced Leopold Bernhard to Hannah one evening at the Dupont Plaza Hotel. It was love at first sight. By this, I do not mean any turn from his beloved wife, Thelma, but rather the immediate sighting of a loved object with no thought of what one is to do about it except to enjoy the moment of meeting. These two were birds of a feather: A brilliant and attractive Berlin Jewess and a Lubeck aristocrat with, as it turned out, a touch of Jewish blood. They spoke in German while I withdrew to watch and marvel at the pleasure they had in each other's company. It was as if they sailed away to a past time and land where thought and taste ruled. It was a delight to see.

They decided to "go out" to a performance of Bach's St. John Passion. Leopold called me the next day and thanked me for the extraordinary experience. He remarked that she was the "quintessential" Berlin lady. The quality of their meeting was in fact the heart and headstone of pre-Nazi Germany and its culture – everything that he and she knew and lived had died with Hitler and the war. The performance of the Passion was faulty, but the evening was wonderful. I don't believe they ever met again.

Hannah called me from New York and asked if I might spend an afternoon with a group of her New School students whom she was sending to Washington for an observation of politics. It was the weekend of an anti-war demonstration when there was real action: *vita activa* in which to participate.

The group of about 10 students came to my home and we talked about neighborhood government, local organizing, workers' councils, the anti-war movement and other exciting issues of political life. One student, Elisabeth Young Bruehl, a beautiful young lady who subsequently wrote Arendt's biography and became a political philosopher in her own right, led the group. This was in 1970.

I met Young-Bruehl two years later when Hannah had arranged for me to give a lecture at Columbia University on urban political life. The subject of my talk was the end of municipal democracy in Boston, based on my scholarly article, "The Disappearance of Municipal Liberty," published in Politics and Society in 1972. The article traced the decision of Boston to move from direct town-meeting government to an elected representative government. I went to New York and delivered my lecture to a large academic audience. Any event sponsored by Hannah Arendt was well attended and received. This was an opportunity for the faculty to have a look at me. During these years of campus revolt, they were in the market for young radical blood to cool student passions. I had no interest in foregoing the freedom of IPS to do what I wished to do for the constraints of an academic life.

I regret that I did not attend Hannah's funeral at Riverside Church. It was unpardonable. Some fundraising reason of urgent concern, which I have long since forgotten, contravened the imperative to attend. What more can I say about this sin of necessity?

In any event, the theologian Robert Jenson asked me to write a Hannah Arendt eulogy for his Lutheran Journal Dialog. I wrote an article that is still quite poignant, drawing heavily on her writings. Barbara Raskin enjoyed it and remarked how beautiful it was. Elisabeth Young-Bruehl appreciated the article. She kindly included me in her biography of Arendt. I touched Hannah's life a bit. She touched mine a great deal. In 1982, I visited Bard College and met President Leon Botstein. I visited the Bard library which housed her private book collection, where I proudly found my book *Neighborhood Government* with her testimonial. I visited her gravesite where she was buried next to her husband. I sat for a long moment in the peacefulness of that setting.

Friendship: David T. Bazelon

"A friend is, as it were, a second self." Marcus Tullius Cicero

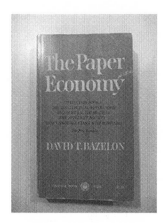

David started his life interested in everything and ended his days interested in nothing. We bonded at the Institute for Policy Studies (IPS) in 1963 and remained talking friends until he died in a nursing home in 2005, sick and ill-tempered. "Don't ask me any more questions. I don't know anything anymore and don't care."

I called him through the years despite his verbal rebuffs. I made a pledge to him years earlier after a terrible argument at IPS, when he was still bold, brilliant, and insolent, that regardless of our arguments and his intellectual abuse I would remain his friend for life. I did this because of his rare brilliance. I knew that I needed his intellectual thought for the rest of my life, and that required my sacrifice of pride. He could yell, scream, dispute and crack mean jokes, but he always said something that was different from what I could learn from others and always made sense to me upon reflection.

David had one arm, three wives, and one child. He grew up in Chicago. He had lost his arm in a street car accident. He wore a prosthetic gloved hand with immovable fingers, although fractal clippers would have made his life easier. He was too vain for that. He was tall and barrel-chested. He had a good head of hair and a decisive face that would have been attractive if his temper was not so caustic. Every time you engaged his eye you were as likely as not to receive the dialectical wag of his sharp tongue. He always was able to say what you said smarter than you said it. Not many people could endure this precision — "What you are really saying is this…." I cherished his preternatural brilliance like a precious gemstone.

David had been a Wall Street lawyer for years before he gave it up for his career as a writer. In those days this meant social criticism for sophisticated magazines like *Commentary, The Partisan Review* and a host of what were then called "little magazines" that paid writers a pittance. He scored big in 1961 with a highly acclaimed book, *The Paper Economy.* (Among his other books were *The Politics of the New Class,* and *Nothing But a Fine Tooth Comb: Essays in Social Criticism.*) David really understood that money was no longer just a tool for the exchange of goods and services. It had become a transactional tool for leveraging assets to build wealth. While we thought that we used money to buy things, the fat cats used money to build wealth.

He understood and abhorred this kind of economy back in the 1960s, foreseeing the emerging inequality of wealth between consumer deadbeats and derivative billionaires. David was a Liberal of the New Deal variety, never a Socialist or Bolshevik. He liked the sturdy yeoman and productive worker and regretted that they were getting stonewalled by slimy lawyers and financiers; and getting soft, compliant, and bemused along the way. In his sharp words, he did not like to see the fat cats screwing the workers, and the workers enjoying being screwed. It was his job to tell everybody the truth about their economic and political illusions and stupidity.

David was an acerbic illusion smasher. That is why he went through three wives, the second who committed suicide, jumping from a New York building. He came to Washington as an IPS Visiting Fellow with a new wife, Mary, who was a neurosurgeon. Mary was on her own track to a Nobel Prize and indulged David until he really got under her skin. She threw him out after three years in Washington and married a rich Jewish businessman who gave her no grief. Instead of "Why are you doing this in that way?" she had a silent rich husband in a fancy house in Woodley Park.

David would always interrupt people in seminars. He was not liked by most of the Fellows because they knew he was smarter than they were, and rude enough to publicly demonstrate it. David, like me, went to the University of Chicago, so I knew his dialectical ways and liked to argue back. Nobody else enjoyed him enough to do this or did not know how to do it. Richard Barnet and Marc Raskin, Co-Directors of IPS, rarely said a word to him. Marc, who brought him to the Institute, always handled him like Clyde Beatty, the circus animal trainer, handled his tigers, at arm's length. Waskow, a mystical Jewish Resident Fellow, was oblivious to his critique. Christopher Jencks, a New England blueblood, and the former editor of *The New Republic,* thought him ill-mannered, and so on and on.

I had a shouting match with Bazelon at a civil rights seminar. I cannot remember the subject or the cause of our argument, but it was a colossal repartee of angry rebuttals that reached a feverish pitch. Fellows and guests were embarrassed at the excitement of our quarrel and became mute and restive. They wanted to leave, but were trapped by our show. The meeting eventually collapsed and we parted. "I never want to talk to you again," were David's singeing words to me.

Later that evening I went to his house. Mary received me and David scowled. "Why are you here?" "I am here because I am your only friend in Washington, if not the world. I intend to remain your friend and talk to you for the rest of your life, regardless of your behavior towards me." He was stunned by the ardent peculiarity of my position. I kept my vow for 42 years, throughout his later tenure at the University of Buffalo, where he went after leaving Washington, and until his death.

Before leaving the Institute he wrote an insightful book, *Power in America*. He defined the New Left more precisely than any writer of his time or since. Young radicals in the 1960s were too enthralled with the excitement of their action to accurately assess the real limit of their political power or its consequences. In short, the 1960s was a masturbatory extravagance. His confreres on the Old Left winced at his sexual innuendoes about the New Left, and the New Left ignored his caution. The book was too brilliant to have any advocates.

He had a girlfriend in his last years when he moved to Madison, Wisconsin. I was the only person beyond his family who communicated with him through all those years, always under the cloud of his bitterness and abuse. None of his honored *Commentary* pals talked to him, so all he had was me, his faithful friend, and Coleman, a son from his marriage with Mary. I committed my friendship to him for life because I needed him for my own intellectual sustenance, and he needed me because every educated friend he ever had, except me, abandoned him.

Lust: Paul Goodman

Lust is best understood as sexual craving and action that is indifferent to social barriers of sexual conduct. We all have sexual desire. Few of us are brazen enough to enact desire beyond the boundaries of reputation and personal safety. For most people sex is normalized. For Paul Goodman, sex was defiant: the more dangerous the encounter, the greater the craving and careless the enactment. It is in this heroic sense of lust that Paul Goodman would define himself as a "queer."

Paul was a Visiting Fellow in the 1963 inaugural year of the Institute for Policy Studies (IPS) in Washington D.C. In his 50s, he was a famous social critic and minor novelist at the time. His book *Growing up Absurd,* was a best-selling social analysis of how organized society distorts the lives of young people, tying them in knots and depriving them of a developing free and purposeful life. The book was a complement to Salinger's, *The Catcher in the Rye.* Both of these books had a lot to do with mobilizing young people in the 1960s to act audaciously rather than respectably.

Paul was born in Greenwich Village and had the New York

Jewish good looks of a young man that turn sallow and creviced when he hits his sixties, which was his age when he arrived at IPS. He was scruffy in his rumpled corduroy pants and shaggy jacket. Paul always smoked a corn cob piper and drooled tobacco juice at the corners of his mouth. Piercing through his horn- rimmed glasses, he spoke slowly and deliberately, revealing a careful and thorough classical education.

Paul moved into a cheap basement apartment at the corner of Connecticut and Florida Avenues, where he lived with his common-law wife of many years. His three children were grown and on their own. The apartment was only a block from IPS.

He was a novelist with his New York trilogy, *Empire City*, a classics teacher at colleges that expelled him for his homosexuality, and a psychotherapist of Gestalt psychology for whom the expression of sexual energy was primary. He was a big name in social criticism at the time, and had just the right éclat that Marc Raskin, IPS director, wanted at his think tank.

Paul avowed his homosexual taste. He liked the adventure of being queer and brought a boy, Johnny, to Washington to live with him and his wife. He got the sex he wanted with his mind and celebrity.

Paul was a thoughtful interlocutor at seminars. He tended to be a monologist, speaking too long and too impatient to listen. His comments were discerning but not exciting. His style and his classical dialectal training would never let a stupid thought rest.

Paul had a penchant for young college boys. They came to the Institute to pick him up and drive him here or there, to lectures and trysts. Paul was never secret about his taste. If sex was relevant to a discussion, he freely mentioned that he was a queer. In those days, he was one of the first notables to out himself. Paul debunked the gay movement. He regarded himself as a queer who enjoyed the adventures and dangers of perversion more than the doldrums of tolerance. He cited the times when he was beaten up. He never thought that a good society could support or withstand a gay culture.

Family, not instinct, was paramount.

His boy Johnny, whom he brought from Antioch College, caused IPS a lot of trouble. He was a good-looking blond-haired kid of 20 years, who, in short order, picked up the rhythm of liberal politics and social change. This was a contentious period of civil rights agitation, anti-war protest, drugs, sex, and a growing left-wing affiliation with decolonized regimes and populist revolutions. As a drug-head love child in an ambiance of social anarchy, Johnny did not take long to see right-wing conspiracies and liberal hypocrisies in every corner. In the company of my accomplished colleagues, Johnny was coy — shy but flirtatious.

I came to the Institute early one morning and was the first to arrive. Western Union delivered a stack of telegrams from newspapers and broadcast stations around the country. The staff came in and the phones started to ring without stop. Jackie Lushin, our office manager, had everyone mobilized on the phones. "No, the Institute is not publishing a scandal sheet of Congressional sex and payoffs." No to this and no to that question! Reporters and photographers came to the door. "No, there is no truth to this announcement. Who is telling you this?"

The "who" was Johnny! Johnny had come to the Institute late the previous night and rifled Christopher Jencks' rolodex of news reporters' names and phone numbers. Christopher had been an editor of the *New Republic* before he joined the Institute. Johnny spent the night alerting reporters that IPS was releasing its first monthly expose of Washington scandal, sex, and corruption. There will be a press conference tomorrow at 4 p.m. at 1901 19th Street, NW.

Every call and telegram was answered. The hoax was contained. While Marc, Dick, and other Fellows and staff were fending off the press, I was busy tracking down Paul to find the whereabouts of Johnny. Paul's wife, the connubial enigma, said that he was with an actor friend who was starring in a Chekhov play at the National Theater.

I raced to the theater and found the hotel where the actor was staying and called him, beseeching him to get Paul to find Johnny and stop the "time bomb." Paul and his thespian friend arrived at the Institute at 3 p.m. Paul had no idea where Johnny was. A few reporters who had not been contacted showed up. In the hustle and bustle of 20 disoriented people, all talking at once, in walked Johnny with the bearing and smile of a conquering hero.

We all lurched towards him, encircling a wild beast with verbal swords. Johnny broke out and moved quickly to Christopher's large desk. He plunged himself into the desk chair and quickly reached for Christopher's long sharp letter opener. Rapier in hand, he said, "If anyone of you comes near me, I'll kill you." We all drew back. Don Michael, Arthur Waskow, Marc Raskin, Richard Barnet, Christopher Jencks, Paul Goodman, his actor friend, and I stood in an arc around the desk at a safe distance from Johnny.

Johnny began a tirade against Paul for deceiving and misusing him. From invective he turned to the rest of us to explain how splendid a project the scandal sheet would be for the Institute. Every placating remark and step forward by one of us was enjoined by Johnny's threat to stand back or he would stab us.

In the next room Jackie called the police. They arrived quickly, but would take no action unless someone made an official complaint. All they saw was a calm young fellow sitting confidently at a desk with a letter opener and surrounded by agitated adults. Paul refused to lodge a complaint, so the cops sat back and watched the show.

It was 5:30 p.m., a half-hour before a scheduled seminar that evening with Theodore Moscoso of the Alliance for Progress. Guests began to arrive, while Johnny held his knife in our faces. Jackie shuffled seminar guests past the madhouse to an upstairs meeting room.

In the midst of this tumult, in walked our IPS fellow Leo Szilard. Leo was a renowned physicist who played a key role in the Manhattan Project atomic bomb development. He was operating his anti-nuclear protest movement from IPS. Leo was a well-practiced refugee. He fled the Nazis for England. He fled England for fear of its weakness to the Nazi onslaught. He was once again in mayhem, and needed to weigh this tumultuous situation. He turned to Johnny sitting regally at the desk with everyone cowering around him and asked, "Johnny, what is going on?"

Johnny explained his plans for the scandal sheet and asked Leo if he would write a monthly article on scandal, sex, and corruption in science circles. "Johnny, I don't think it (v)ill (v)ork." Forever escaping, he turned on his heels and left the room.

Then Arthur Waskow, who became a rabbi later in life, said some soothing words to Johnny. At that moment of sentiment, Johnny dropped his guard and I pounced on him and grabbed the blade. Everyone moved in for the kill and we soon grounded Johnny.

With Johnny subdued, but still violent, Paul said that he had to leave to give a speech at Howard University. "Not on your life" I snapped. "You are going to take responsibility for Johnny. File a complaint so the cops can take him" "No, I will not," he truculently replied. "It is against my anarchist principles." The police looked on in amusement.

I asked one of the secretaries to get a cab. A cab had just dropped off a guest for the seminar and waited for us. We tied Johnny's hands and forced him on the backseat floor of the cab. I declared that we were taking Johnny to the hospital." Paul assented and he, his actor friend, Arthur and I drove off to D.C. General Hospital pinioned on Johnny's back.

The hospital gave Johnny a sedative and told us to take him directly to St. Elizabeth's, the psychiatric hospital of Washington. We did, and deposited him and Paul in the emergency psychiatric room. I remember the yellow lock up room into which they deposited the boy. Arthur and I left Paul to deal with details.

The next day Paul asked me for a favor. He was leaving town for a lecture tour and would be gone for a week. Would I check in with Johnny to see how he was doing? I visited Johnny a few days later. He was remarkably calm. He had harsh words for Paul and asked me for some cigarette money. I gave him 10 dollars.

When Paul returned the following week I mentioned that I visited Johnny and that he seemed alright. I asked him for my 10 dollars. "You should not have given him anything." I never saw my money and reflected on a comment that Paul had made months earlier about the many times he had been beaten in pursuit of his sexual pleasures. The punishment was part of the prize!

For Paul, sex was a jungle hunt. He pursued his prey for lust, not love. Affection was only a tactic of capture. Whatever happened to him or his prey was the law of the jungle. If he was beaten or his prey was strait-jacketed in an insane asylum, it was all part of the sport. He compartmentalized his life into two parts — intellectual and beast — and saw no contradiction. Johnny was jungle meat. It never occurred to Paul that he had a civilized responsibility for the boy. If I gave Johnny $10, that was my problem, not Paul's responsibility. Why coddle dead meat? Paul had a fine mind and raw appetite.

Johnny never appeared again at the Institute. I never asked Paul what happened to Johnny. It would be asking a hunter standing before the taxidermied head of a tiger, what happened to the rest of the tiger?

Desolation: Ramparts Magazine

We celebrate leaders of radical movements. But there is always a dark side to good causes. Scams lurk beneath the surface. This is a story of moral turpitude.

In the mid-1960s to 1975, *Ramparts Magazine* was the mouthpiece of the New Left. Warren Hinckle took over a sleepy Catholic social policy journal with 2,500 subscribers, owned by Edward Keating, and turned it into a fiery mass circulation left-wing magazine that reached a peak of 400,000 subscribers in the mid-1970s.

Hinkle promised that every issue would be a bombshell. It published Che Guevara's diaries, with a long introduction by Fidel Castro; Eldridge Cleaver's letters from prison; a photo essay in January 1967 showing the injuries inflicted on Vietnamese children by American bombs. He blew the cover of the CIA's funding the

National Student Association, the A.F.L.-C.I.O., Encounter magazine and the Partisan Review. Warren told the Washington Post in 1981, "What journalism is about is to attack everybody. First you decide what's wrong, then you go out to find the facts to support that view, and then you generate enough controversy to attract attention."

I first met Warren Hinckle in 1965, when he and his team came to Washington to make their anti-Vietnam War mark on the nation's capital. Warren was a big, blustering fellow with a daunting eye patch. He invited the Institute for Policy Studies (IPS) to a lavish bash on the entire top floor of the Hay Adams Hotel. There may have been close to a hundred people there – writers, politicians, intellectuals, and protest leaders.

Hinckle and his staff flew in from Europe because of an airline strike. They could not get from their office in San Francisco to Washington, D.C, so they flew around the world to get to the Hay Adams at a staggering travel cost, not to mention the bathtubs of champagne, booze, oysters, and shrimp that the hotel staff wheeled into the party. It was a boisterous affair and people were plastered.

I met Edward Keating, an industrial heir and owner and publisher of *Ramparts*. He was a serious man, a bit flustered at the extravagance of the event. He had paid the price of hiring Hinckle to remake the magazine into a kettledrum of protest action. Warren put Ed through a financial wringer to transform the magazine. Later in his life Warren briefly edited *City of San Francisco*, a magazine owned by Francis Ford Coppola. According to Newsweek, "Insiders joke that Hinckle is the only man who can spend money faster than Coppola can make it." Ed got Warren's first financial drubbing. Warren was a profligate spender of other people's money.

Warren asked Marc to select an IPS Fellow who could be the Washington editor of *Ramparts*. Marc recommended me. Warren and I met and he told me that he needed hot stories from the political ground of Washington, where the policies were made, where scandals reside, and where the protests were taking place. I would enlist top writers at a set price, and he would publish their pieces and pay them. I received no compensation, which was okay with me. I had my salary from the Institute and our dissent was aligned. At the time, I was a contributor to *Liberation* magazine.

For a year I recruited authors and articles for *Ramparts*. These were fine pieces by prominent writers. The trouble was that Warren did not pay their bills. I was hounded by these authors, some of whom were friends living their piecework lives.

I kept calling Warren to pay the writers. He said he would and never did. I decided to fly to San Francisco and settle the matter with Warren. He was pleased to receive me for lunch at a fancy seafood restaurant. We were joined by Bob Scheer, his associate editor and a very nice fellow. Bob was meek next to his titanic boss.

"Margaritas for all," Warren declared to the waiter. We chitchatted about politics and the war and the drinks passed quickly down Warren's gullet. "Another round," he entreated.

"What new articles are you arranging?"

"Warren, that is why I'm here! You have to pay the writers for their articles over the past year."

"Of course I will! Another round of margaritas!" he blared. I demurred.

"What are they complaining about? *Ramparts* is a great forum for them and they should be proud of their work for the "Movement!"

"Warren, you know they live on income from their articles. You are a journalist!"

"Hmmm, he mused, "another round!"

He looked at me with an inebriated and berating eye. "The anti-war movement needs their ideas and inspiration. Get them on board! They will be paid."

"When"? I implored. "What can I tell them to make them believe me? I can't enlist new articles until writers of past published articles are paid."

"A strong person makes sacrifices" he blared. "They are complainers and weak. You have to motivate them. Are you too weak to do it? … Another round!"

By his fifth margarita Warren declared that I was a coward and traitor. Thereupon, I resigned my position to the bloviating editor of *Ramparts*. The writers never saw the money. But I did learn the power of the "Movement" to browbeat common sense, and that the best defense against this moral fraudulence was retreat.

In 1967, I received a call from Ed Keating. We had kept in touch about the payment demands that burdened me. "Could you please come and see me. I will pay for your air ticket." I agreed and flew to California and met Ed in a Menlo Park motel. Here was the scion of industrial wealth meeting me in a second-rate motel.

Ed thanked me from coming. He began distraught and ended in tears. "Warren has ruined me. He has bled me dry. I feel terrible about not paying your writers, but I am broke." I felt sorry for Ed, but there was nothing that I could do. Warren skinned him alive. *Ramparts* went on with new investors until its bankruptcy in 1975. Warren went onto to other journalistic scams, bleeding soft- hearted rich guys until he died in 2016. This was the end of my journalistic management responsibilities, and the writers whom I enlisted took it on the chin. They had been through this before. Warren manifested the unscrupulous underbelly of "Movement" magazines that exploit their owners and ardent writers.

Extortion: General Saraka

Having been to Mississippi and organized black neighborhood organizations in Columbus, Chicago, Boston, Pittsburgh and other cities, I had a reputation among my white colleagues of the Institute for Policy Studies (IPS) for knowing black people. Jim Ridgeway, an IPS Fellow and a contributing editor of the *New Republic* and *The Village Voice*, asked me one day to accompany him to interview a new black leader on the scene in Washington, General Saraka of the Blackman's Liberation Force.

Washington, New York, Chicago, Berkeley, California, and other urban liberal hub cities were abuzz with Black Nationalism. This concept was promulgated by Malcolm X, who was assassinated in 1964, and picked up by Stockley Carmichael, Black Muslims, Black Panthers, the Symbionese Liberation Army and a plethora of militant fringe groups, each with a leader seeking publicity, money, and recruits. One such group was the Blackman's Liberation Force.

We took a cab to a storefront on 14th and Kennedy Streets, NW, and walked up a flight of stairs. We were received by a uniformed guard with a rifle, and escorted into the office of General Saraka. Saraka was a tall handsome man in an immaculate military uniform. Several aides were in the room and we were seated. A young women in African dress served us coffee. "We only use brown sugar."

Jim went through his questions, discomforted by the brace of weapons that surrounded him. I said very little. Saraka prattled his answers in stentorian tone about his black force's mission to provide armed service to the decolonized states of Africa so they could remain free of American and European scoundrels who had enslaved them. He dodged the question of which regimes invited his assistance. He was now building and training his forces. He needed financial support for this noble task, which he likened to the armed forces of Israel Zionism in defense of their homeland. He was recruiting derelict and mischievous young men on the streets of Washington and other cities for disciplined training and valiant service. I got the hint. He wanted good press in the *New Republic,* but had no understanding of the negative sensationalist twists of journalism.

Jim wrote a colorful piece because there was little substance in the matter. He portrayed Saraka as a hustler and his "force" as a ridiculous nonce. Several weeks passed without any response from Saraka.

Oddly enough, I got the response. Saraka called me to invite me to come to his office on
Kennedy Street alone. I declined and said that he could come to my office at IPS if he wanted to see me, but without an armed guard. He showed up the next day late in the afternoon.

After some pleasantries, Saraka withdrew a letter and a check from his brief case and laid them before me. "I don't want to cash this check." I read the letter from Willis Carto on the letterhead of the Anti-Semitic Liberty Lobby thanking Saraka for his proposed article for Spotlight, "How the Jews Betrayed Me." It was full of flattery praising Saraka for his courage in revealing Jewish treachery and Zionist cabals. Carto asked him to accept the enclosed check for $2,000 for the article. I knew of Carto and had a Chicago brush-in with George Lincoln Rockwell, the American Nazi leader in the 1950s. Saraka was in with a rough crowd.

"So don't write the article and cash the check," I replied.

"I will not cash it if you can get me a Jewish check for $2, 000," he submitted.

"You will cash it anyway and what Jewish money are you talking about?"

"You know the Jewish leaders." In fact, I was on the Urban Affairs Committee of the American Jewish Committee and had attended several meetings without getting to know any moneyed Jews in the Jewish defense arena. He apparently had done some research, but not enough. The rich Jews that I knew were supporters of IPS and they had a different agenda than opposing anti-Semitism; I certainly knew they would not kowtow to this low grade extortion.

"I don't know the kind of rich Jewish leaders that you are looking for, and if I did I wouldn't bring your two-bit shakedown to their attention. We are finished. You can get up and leave." He hemmed and hawed and made another feint try. I got up and showed him the door. He left and I never expected to see him again.

The following year Saraka turned to another scheme. He was transformed into a public advocate of methadone. I heard him promote his scheme at the Potter's House café on Columbia Road, where charlatans were always welcomed as long as they pronounced a politically correct line. Saraka was funded by the District Government to wage a war on heroin, no less difficult then the military defense of decolonized Africa. After this event I never heard about him. Like a weasel, he vanished from the scene.

A Gift of the Gods: Sam Rosenkrantz

The ancients were wise to have a god of laughter, Gelos. Humans need merriment. Gelos travelled to German in the nominative *gelachter* and participle *lachan,* and to Yiddish in *gelekhter* and *lakhn.* Gelos is joined by the hip to Comus, the god of festivity, revelry and anarchy. Comus travelled to France as *Comédien;* to Germany as *Comiker;* to the Yiddish world as *Kamidyan;* and to the English world as *Comedian,* personified by Falstaff the Court Fool.

Laughter and its agent comedy are divine spirits that all people crave. In our anarchic youth laughter careens through the landscape of our life. In mid-age it delights our intelligence. In mature age, it nests beneath the scope of sober responsibilities. In old age, it withdraws and we beckon to retrieve its merriment.

Old men cannot drum up the spirit of laughter, but they can remember their great comic friends. This is a tale of memory. Sam Rosenkrantz was the greatest spirit of laughter in my life and my generation of friends. He was an irresistible comedic genius who selflessly blessed his friends with cracking mirth.

My friend Ron Grossman of the Chicago Tribune wrote a
poignant eulogy to Sam's comedic spirit.

> *"He poured forth a torrent of words, shifting between metaphysics and
> slapstick, larding the King's English with Yiddish expressions. We
> met at the University of Chicago, where flower children studied the
> classics of antiquity. He had an infectious sense of life's absurdity.*
>
> *His bittersweet anecdotes would seem improbable, if told by anyone
> else. With him, you'd say: "Sam, only you'd have a cockamamie
> adventure like that."*

Sam and I met in 1967 in Mandel Hall court at the University of
Chicago and were closest friends in Washington, D.C., until his death
in 2017. No more than 50 students lolled on the grassy turf enjoying
Louie Armstrong's ensemble. It is unbelievable today that students
back then could casually hear the supreme brilliance of Louie
Armstrong singing and braying "St. Louie Woman" and "Chinatown,
My Chinatown" at no ticket cost. Sam was accompanied by Janet
Langan, who soon became his wife, forever. I was joined by my
girlfriend Dottie, who soon after became my wife for one year. Other
friends were present, including Jerry Boime, Larry Rosenberg, and
Lee Haupt to enjoy the radiant music, not realizing the uniqueness of
this blessed period of the American cultural renaissance in the 1950s.
Today, an idol of Armstrong's stature would fill a stadium of 50,000
people at ticket prices in the hundreds.

The 1950s was simply a generation of small scale life before the
commercialization of live music. We would walk to the black jazz
clubs on 63rd street and hear Ella Fitzgerald and Thelonious Monk
for the price of a beer. We would visit the Second City pub on 57th
street to see Mike Nichols, Elaine May, and the whole Second City
Improv gang for the price of a beer and no cover charge.

The University of Chicago under the leadership of Robert
Maynard Hutchins was the epitome of American intellectual
education. Roaming the campus were Paul Tillich, Leo Strauss,
Enrico Fermi, Hans Morgenthau, Hannah Arendt, Saul Bellows,
Marc Chagall, David Riesman, Milton Friedman, and a host of

American and European cultural luminaries. Flanking Chicago were the literary and artistic epicenters of New York and the mélange of musical and cinematic masters in Los Angeles.

The whole country was vibrant with new thought, art, and science; all in counterpoise with the Red Scare of Senator Joseph McCarthy (R-WI) and the Korean War. America is always best when it fights the harassment and doldrums of convention. There were no greater fighters than men like Robert Maynard Hutchins who spoke truth to power; and there was no better time for satire. This decade was Sam's stage for his life of comedy. It was shared by Mort Sahl, Lenny Bruce, Buddy Hackett, and Jackie Masson, all pros. But Sam the amateur was the best.

A circle of good minds and young bodies were drawn to Sam like bees to nectar. Sam was short, chunky and good looking, in a Jewish sort of way. He had a brilliant mind, but all of this intellectual juice was strained through a comedic filter. The dregs of argumentation were swept away, leaving the honey of pure mental and physical satire. We were a field of clover. Our nectar kept him and all of us going for hours on end and even days; in fact for a lifetime.

Our laughter was as physical as his comedy. As he attacked the barricade of stupidity, we laughed until our sides were splitting. Day passed to night and night to morning without a break of Sam's manic burlesque.

We enjoyed memorable events, like our spin to Cape Cod for a weekend at Peggy Lee's house; our audience with Marlon Brando at the Pump Room at the Ambassador East Hotel; our summer cottage on Lake Michigan at the Indiana Dunes; our evening at the Gate of Horn when Lenny Bruce was arrested for obscenity; our burlesque at the trial of Nazi leader George Lincoln Rockwell; Sam's fistfight inaugural induction to Second City; a weeklong Peyote fantasy; and banana splits with Marc Chagall.

Sam was born in Chicago. When his mother died in his teens, his father Louis sent him to his grandparents on the Lower East Side of New York City to raise him with *Yiddishkeit*. He developed the convoluted analytical mind of a *Yeshiva bucher* and the spirit of a *borsht belt* wit. When he returned to Chicago to live with his father and brothers, he was as tormented by the contempt of his educated immigrant father, Louis Rosenkrantz, who scorned his foolishness. Sam never had enough confidence to become a professional comedian, so he escaped and joined the Air Force.

Louis was a teacher in Russia who fled the pogroms for Chicago and settled for a small grocery store beneath the "L" tracks on Chicago's Southside. After Sam's mother died, Louis married a rich Jewish widow with lots of property and returned to his past honors. He retired from cabbage and pickles and lived on the bounty of his new wife, Rose, to become a student in Slavic Language Studies at the University of Chicago. Louis became the intellectual dandy of his dreams and brought cookies every day to the tea room at the divinity school to charm young female scholars. His presence on the campus was a constant torment for Sam, who was also at the university after leaving the air force and a stint at the University of Illinois.

Sam ambled around the campus, trying this and that while holding on to odd jobs in catering events and at the Chicago stockyards. He was devoted to his wife Janet, a rebellious suburban Catholic girl from Naperville, who fell in love with this comedic Jew. Were it not for Janet's care, Sam would have died after his first massive stroke a decade ago. They had two children, Max and Elizabeth.

There are several episodes with Sam at the University that I want to record because they were unique to the generation of the 1950s and early 1960s. The first has to do with George Lincoln Rockwell, the American Nazi leader of the 1950s.

Anti-Semitism did not vanish after the end of the World War II and the Holocaust. It simply became more socially silent and publically outrageous. The Jew hatred of my youth had much more to do than with Catholic Church loathing that the Jews had killed Christ. It was imbued within society to the extent that the gentile guys and gals on our city block feared a Jewish contagion. After the war anti-Semitism in the U.S. became secular, as it was in Germany during the rise of Hitler. The Jews controlled this! The Jews controlled that! Anti-Semitism became more economic – from blood lust to money clout. It is the same today, but to a lesser extent, at least I hope so!

Sam, and Jerry Boime, my political science classmate, and I visited the trial of George Lincoln Rockwell in 1960. Rockwell had held a

July 4th anti-Semitic rally that resulted in a fracas and Rockwell's arrest. When we entered courtroom, other than a small phalanx of his followers, we found only a handful of people present. We had our choice of the best seats.

Once the proceeding commenced, Rockwell strode to the witness stand and went through a cursory swearing in. Following the judge's procedural questions, Rockwell, without legal counsel, proceeded to hurl a series of anti-Semitic bolts. The judge, angry and flustered, attempted to silence Rockwell. It was a short trial. Rockwell tried to shout down the judge and was physically removed from the court room. As Rockwell and his pals were removed they passed our seats. Rockwell peered at us — three physiognomic Jews, and roared at Sam, "You, Jew boy, we're going to put you on the front cover of our next issue." What a literary angel! Having no Ant-Nazi magazine of our own, we collectively said, "Fuck you!"

We shared a police event in 1962. Lenny Bruce was performing at the Gate of Horn dinner club and Sam, Jerry, Dale, and I went to see the show. Bruce was a political stand-up comedian at a time when the Left was craving for a Star to stand up to Red Scares, politicians who tried to topple Castro, and to city leaders like Mayor Daley who devoured their fiefdoms.

That night Bruce went after the Pope and the priests. Mind you, this was roughly five decades before the pederast church scandals broke into the public eye and the courts. There had always been rumors of sexual hanky-panky, but nothing went public in those days of political and media protection. Bruce embroidered the rumors and made hilarious fantasy and hypocrisy out of a reality of which neither he nor we knew the real stuff. As we guffawed, Bruce built on his momentum until the audience reached a high pitch of hilarity. At that moment the lights of the club went on and no less than two dozen cops entered of the hall. They commanded everyone to rise and stand in place, while they cordoned off the entire ballroom with yellow tape. "You are all under arrest for indecency. You will march in single file to the exit, where you will be escorted into police wagons for legal proceedings." We were astounded by the sheer anomaly of the raid.

We were directed to the street and saw a dozen paddy wagons waiting. Were it not for a few lawyers in the audience, who made vehement protest that menaced the police, we would have been driven to jail. As it was, only Bruce was arrested. The customers were let free, but set free with a thought. We had participated in what Mayor Daley and the cops viewed as a lethal insult and destructive attack on the Catholic Church, the Pope in Rome, and the Archdiocese of Chicago. We were blasphemers, and as such deserved the punishment of ages past, only mitigated by modern protections of free speech. The only thing that the Mayor Daley could get away with was to scare the shit out of us and please the parishes. I was never protected by the police from anti-Semitic slurs, but was now suborned by papist police protection. This was the first time that I really felt like a Negro, subjected to arbitrary police action.

Off to Provincetown, Cape Cod. My father gave me his Plymouth car in 1959: and Sam, Jerry and I drove it from Chicago to Provincetown. A friend of ours knew Peggy Lee, who had a summer house there, arranged for us to board free of charge for two weeks. Sam drove nonstop all night until we arrived at this artistic haven. We did not know a soul, nor did we have the faintest idea of what a vacation was. In those days, Provincetown was a watering hole for artists and writers. It had not yet become a gay Mecca. It was a small town with basically nothing to do, unless you were an artist or writer and could work and drink with your artist and writer friends. We moseyed around the town and beach, but spent most of our time indulging in the fantasies of an opulent beach house, amusing ourselves listening to jazz records. After three days of empty meandering, we left and drove back to Chicago. The point of this story is simply that the 1950s was simply a time when nobodies like us could land in Peggy Lee's home. The celebrity of entertainment was much less pronounced that the celebrity of intellectual scholarship, fine art, classical music, and science. Who was Peggy Lee next to Picasso?

Movie stars ranked high, but they were not esteemed. In 1962, we were invited, with free admission, to the Ambassador East Hotel Pump Room for a press conference by Marlon Brando for his new film, "The Ugly American." There he was in the flesh, talking to a few journalists and students like us who responded to a posted university notice of the event. Jerry's brother, Al, was there with Sam, Janet, her roommate, Myra, and me. We were seated at one of the curving brocaded booths, just like rich people, and given a menu from which we ordered beer and a nosh.

Brando spoke blandly about the movie and about himself. The Pump Room tables had a hook up for telephones at the table. Our friend Myra nonchalantly called her girlfriend to tell her that she could not play bridge that night. Al Boime, Jerry's brother, an expert on Delacroix, was so impressed by the visual image of Myra's call from the Pump Rom that he fell in love with her. They were married a few years later.

As for drugs, Aldous Huxley's 1954 book, *The Doors of Perception,* exposed us to the psychedelic realm. It was legal to order Peyote from Mrs. Wright's Cactus farm in Texas. The price was about $15. Sam, Janet, Dottie. Jerry, and I received a large package in the mail and opened it for our first and my last Peyote party. It was foul smelling vegetable matter on arrival, but once we washed it, mashed it into chocolate chip dough and baked it, the cookies were edible. It packed a punch. After a short while, I perceived a new and fantastic visual and sound world. It was an isolating experience that in my case, lasted for four days. The last day was horrible and psychotic. I remember sitting in Gorden's restaurant on 57th Street and looking at each face with paranoiac fear. By the fourth day, my metabolism eliminated the last vestige of this awful stuff. I never took it again. Several of my friends had a benign experience and took the stuff again and again. But it was not for me. It was more than my psyche could handle.

It is hard for today's graduate students to believe that I left for the University of Chicago in 1963 after 12 years with a student debt of $200. It was a different age. My friends and I were supported by scholarships and fellowships during our entire tenure at the university. I never had to approach my parents for support money. I was even able to get married and live in a decent apartment on my project and teaching earnings.

The bottom line was that we lived in a robust economy where things cost very little. Before my departure from Chicago, the rent on my last four-room apartment on 54th Place and University Avenue was only $37 a month. A hamburger was 40 cents; coffee a dime; cigarettes were 15 cents a pack; and a high class downtown dinner was available for $3.00.

The epitome of this economic largesse was a beachfront cottage in the Indiana Dunes that Sam, Janet, and I rented in 1962 for the entire summer season for $375. It was a dump but accommodated us with bedrooms, kitchen, living room and an open air breezy porch.

Jerry Boime and I were taking Ed Shils' course on politics and technology, which met on Monday and Wednesday. After class on Wednesday, we drove one hour to the cottage and stayed until Monday morning. The cottage porch led directly to our Lake Michigan beach. We enjoyed a summer of blessed water. We invited friends to join in this joy and had a memorable summer of swimming, rock and roll music, philosophical discourse, beer, Sam's slap stick comedy and bonhomie. At the end of that summer, we all prevailed on Sam to go back to the University of Illinois and complete his degree, which he did.

Sam and Janet joined me in Washington, D.C., in 1965 for a Capitol hayride for the rest of his life. I brought him into the Institute for Policy Studies (IPS), where Marc Raskin gave him a gracious stipend to liven up boring seminars. Sam bombarded the political scene, delighting big thinkers and big shots. Our patron Ed Jans hired him for the opening act at his new Snow Mass resort in Colorado.

My friend, W.H. Ferry (Ping), was so elated by Sam' comedy, that he hired a recording studio to tape Sam for a California radio station performance. Ping, Marc, Janet and I sat in to watch Sam go blank. Not a word!

There was a riotous event at Lee Webb' wedding party at a the Museum of Modern Art in D.C. The museum, which is now defunct, was established by our IPS patron Phil Stern, heir of Sears Roebuck. Lee Webb, a Fellow at IPS, was a boastful leader in Students for a Democratic Society (SDS), who never won Sam Rosenkrantz's affection. Lee married a rich New York gal, Marilyn Salzman. All of us were invited to the wedding reception hosted by Marilyn's dazzling family. Her bejeweled and patronizing aunt moseyed over to our group and asked Sam, "Young man, what do you do?" Sam replied, "I do this," and stuck his pinky finger in her champagne glass. She was appalled, "How dare your impudence!" He stared keenly at her cosmetic face and said, "And I dare this!" To wit, he shoved his hand into the wedding cake and plastered her face with a fistful of whipped cream." Arghh, arghh," she shrieked. Her brothers came running to us like attack dogs. We fled to the street and hightailed it back home. This was one step further than Charlie Chaplain had ever gone. Sam one-upped the Little Tramp.

After this incident, Sam's presence at IPS withered. He had to find a salaried job. He landed one selling ads for the *Washington Jewish Week*. There he met Danny Kushner, with whom he worked for the next 30 years. Sam and Danny sold windows, like Rodney Dangerfield did on his way up the comedy ladder. They were a great team. Sam would cold call with a comic connivance to capture his respondent. They all took the bait and wanted more guffaws with Sam. He would charm them at the starting gate and win them with follow up calls of infectious wit. Danny would take over for the close. Sam sowed. Danny reaped

Years of cold calling sharpened and broadened Sam's comic portfolio. He had to prepare each call with a timely trop. 'Hello, Mrs. Katz. Are you aware of the burglary on your block last week?"

"No I wasn't informed. Are you the police?"

"I am not the police, but the police informed me of the burglary. The entry was through the widow. Are your windows secured?"

"I don't know."

"Can my company visit and take a look … for your safety?"

Sam died in 2016 following his fifth stroke. He was my closest friend in Washington, D.C. Oddly enough, each stroke degraded his cognitive faculties, but enhanced his physical comedy. His comedy was a divine gift. He entertained the folks in the nursing homes in his last years. He was lucky to return home for periods of Janet's loving care; but always another stroke to the final sendoff of Gelos, back to the gods.

Prometheus: Karl Hess

To the reader who does not believe that the ancient gods visit us and dwell awhile, here is evidence to the contrary. When I was at the Institute for Policy Studies (IPS) in Washington, D.C., Prometheus appeared in 1965 in the person of Karl Hess.

First, a reminder of Prometheus, "a Titan, culture hero, and trickster figure who is credited with the creation of man from clay, and who defies the gods by stealing fire and giving it to humanity, an act that enabled progress and civilization. Prometheus is known for his intelligence and as a champion of mankind." (William Hansen, *Classical Mythology: A Guide to the Mythical World of the Greeks and Romans*)

Karl arrived at IPS on a motorcycle with a leather jacket and a goatee. Marc Raskin, IPS Director, had learned about this notable 42 year-old figure, who came from the right-wing to the left-wing in a flash of time after Senator Barry Goldwater (R-AZ) defeat by President Lyndon B. Johnson in the 1964 election. Marc invited Karl to join us as a Visiting Fellow. Anyone who had the rhetorical finesse to write the famous Goldwater declamation: *"I would remind you that extremism in the defense of liberty is no vice. And let me remind you also that moderation in the pursuit of justice is no virtue,"* was fair game for a young and assertive think tank.

Karl left the Republican Party and became an anti-Vietnam radical. He left his suit and tie behind, and adopted the style of a delayed Hippie. He joined the Students for A Democratic Society (SDS) and strove to bring right-wing libertarians together with anti-government left-wing dissidents like Carl Oglesby of the free speech movement at Berkeley. He continued the fight against the draft, which he initiated in the Goldwater camp of the Republican Party, a goal finally achieved under Nixon, whom Karl despised.

At the IPS seminars Karl propounded anarchist and libertarian theories and practices, chief of which was his refusal to pay federal income taxes. He never abridged this refusal until his dying day. He was against the State and for community life and personal self-reliance. As a Fellow, he avidly supported my work on neighborhood government, and applied this affinity to the Adams Morgan neighborhood in which we lived.

He and his wife, Therese, had a walk up apartment on commercial 18th Street. He was born in this neighborhood and now was determined to reside in it as a political citizen. Since he could no longer earn taxable wages, he took up trade skills, like welding and electrical work to barter his services for personal needs. He became an excellent welder and was sought for industrial and artistic work.

Along with others, like Marie Nahikian and Topper Carew, Karl and I organized the Adams Morgan Neighborhood government (AMO) and fought numerous issues of development, discrimination, public services, and education against the city council, zoning board, local banks and real estate developers. I applied my work in neighborhood government to structure AMO as a direct and deliberative neighborhood assembly. We organized the neighbors and had many meetings with hundreds of citizen residents in attendance.

We supported a neighborhood cooperative grocery store with a wider selection of healthy foods, far healthier than the foods that the local Safeway provided. We supported Topper Carew's New Thing center that was a national milestone in black arts and culture. We had volunteer personal services groups that helped the elderly and infirm handle daily life at no cost. The neighborhood was rip-roaring in local self-reliance, self-help and entertainment. Karl and Therese were key figures in imbedding the spirit of E.F. Schumacher's program of *Small is Beautiful* and an ambiance of autonomy to the Adams Morgan community.

The most remarkable innovation was Karl's experimentation with neighborhood technology. Like Prometheus, Karl brought fire and food to the neighborhood's mankind. He occupied an abandoned factory on Kalorama Road, and with a crew of young techies turned the place into a laboratory for neighborhood technology. His group did early work turning solar energy into electricity for lighting and heating. He developed the first large scale indoor field for growing edible bean sprouts. In short order, many homes in the neighborhood were following suit with their own basement mini-plantations. His team produced liquid soap that was distributed for a pittance to residents for detergent and hand use. The boldest task was the construction of enormous tanks in the factory for fish culture. The tanks were filled with hundreds of trout. This was one of the first scale applications of indoor fish farming in the county. It thrived until it was destroyed by vandalism; and with that wanton destruction and the remorse of dead trout our neighborhood technology regime came to an end. Karl and Therese pulled up stakes and left the city.

Karl and Therese had several break-ins to their apartment. These were high crime times in Washington. There were a lot of poor households and destitute people in the neighborhood. We were not naïve about robbery, riots, and lootings. We had our share before, during and after the assassination of Martin Luther King in 1968.

Karl was no babe in the woods and bore the anxiety of the danger like everyone else. But he could not understand or tolerate wanton vandalism. It is one thing to see people loot Columbia Avenue stores for food, clothes, appliances, and liquor. This stuff was useful to people. But to smash ingenious fish tanks and homemade technology equipment for no material purpose was a nihilism that Karl could not tolerate. Karl and Therese decided to move to the country in West Virginia. We beseeched him to the stay, but to avail.

AMO continued for several years without Karl, but our spirit declined. The god who affronted power and stole fire from the good for his beloved mankind was gone. Following a protracted dead zone of community activity, gentrification set in. The black people and white urban geeks were displaced and low rent housing gave way to million dollar homes. And why did our glory pass? For two reasons: a desultory city government that was too obliging to political correctness and did not protect the property of our creative community; and the rapacious reach of real estate developers and home owners for more and more property value.

Karl and Therese bought some land in Kerneysville, West Virginia, and built a home on a hillock. They carved out 2,000 square feet of living space with an earthen roof and back side, and frontal glass panels overlooking their wetland field and stream. They met new country friends and continued community work for local self-reliance. Karl became more famous as a mint mark for libertarian thought and action. He wrote a number of well received books, including his own auto biographies, *Dear America* and *Mostly on Edge*.

I maintained friendly contact with Karl and Therese. I brought my wife and kids to their country place and we continued the good times and talk that we had in the city. When his heart finally gave out, he chose a perilous course of early stage heart transplants. He eventually passed. I gave a eulogy at his memorial service in their country arbor.

Karl was a rare philosopher who actually practiced what he preached. He had a rational and scientific mind. Nothing ever deflected him from reason. Thought, independence and conviction were his mark.

Philosophy has always had a tug of war between *logos* and *bios,* word and lived life. Nietzsche referenced this paradox, noting: *The only critique of a philosophy that is possible and that proves anything, namely trying to see whether one can live in accordance with it, has never been taught at universities; all that had ever been taught is a critique of words by means of other words."*

Karl was a man of words and actions that gave truth to his words. At his root, he had a powerful defiant individual spirit. He may have got this from his mother, who left her adulterous husband, refused child support, and raised Karl on the wage of a telephone operator.

Wherever it came from, he lived a promethean life tricking great power and was reverent only to reason. He also paid the price of Prometheus, the vengeful taxing government eagle daily pecking at his liver for his defiance; and worst of all, mollycoddling vandals who destroyed his technology gifts to a neighborhood's mankind.

Sweet Reason: Hilda Ellison

We tend to think of political liberty as bold actions by grand figures in dark times. There is a drive for liberty by ordinary people on behalf of their community in bright times. This is a story of a simple woman whose sense of liberty was released in magnificent prudence in service to the governance of her neighborhood community.

When I first came to visit Pastor Leopold Bernhard and his neighborhood of the First English Lutheran Church in Columbus Ohio in 1965, he brought me to a spare cottage home to meet Hilda Ellison, one of his church leaders. Hilda was a black lady about 60. She stood no more than five feet in height and weighed about 350 pounds. She was seated in a well-worn easy chair astride bags of clothes and mending items. She had a cane at her side and had the sweetest face, an expression as soft as cotton, and a mind as strong as steel. Hilda was a laundress.

"Welcome Pastor, can John get you some tea?" John was Hilda's husband, a frail and nervous old coot.

"Hilda, I want you to meet Mr. Kotler from Washington. He is going to help us organize the neighborhood to run the church community center. "By time", she remarked, "that the folks take responsibility for the place."

For the next two years I stayed many evenings in one of her upstairs bedrooms. Hilda had not been upstairs for years, but she managed to descend to her cellar, where she canned vegetables and fruits and prepared the best canned spicy corn that I have ever tasted.

As we organized the East Central Citizens Organization (ECCO) neighborhood government over the next five years, Hilda played a key leadership role. She was proud of her neighborhood government.

In 1967, I travelled with Hilda Ellison and three other members of ECCO to Boston to visit the Columbia Point Community Health

Center, which the Ford Foundation had established as a model "Grey Areas" medical project. This as a splendid facility, and our folks were mightily impressed. We were then planning our ECCO medical office and wanted to see the first model community health center in the country.

ECCO's territorial community encompassed one square mile in Columbus. Its boundaries included 5,000 black residents, with a few white folks still remaining. ECCO was organized as a 501(c)(3) tax exempt and tax deductible entity and was governed by the direct assembly of its residents, who elected executive officers. All budgets, bylaws, and programs were decided by direct assembly. The elected officers implemented and administered these decisions.

ECCO was developed by me, Leopold Bernhard, and a team of neighborhood leaders as an experiment in urban neighborhood government. It was funded directly by several federal government agencies for youth programs, job training and placement, housing assistance, elderly care, and a host of community development activities. Its aim was to take over and govern the physical assets of the First English Lutheran Church Community Center that housed these programs. That goal was reached.

The Boston center staff received us with enthusiasm and pride in their modern facility located in a dismal public housing project. It was serving a large population, much larger than ECCO's 5,000 residents. We met with the doctors and administrators. They were very helpful in explaining everything. Hilda was the leader of our group.

After two hours of presentation and discussion, Hilda declared that she did not want "All this kind of stuff." ECCO needed a storefront medical office with a night doctor. The medical staff was puzzled. Doctors worked during the day and it would be very difficult to find a night practitioner.

Why in the world would she want to forego this kind of modern service facility? She resisted. "When folks come home from work, that's when they find that their kids are sick. We need a doctor that works at night. That's when we need him." They retorted, "Where can you find such a person?" She replied, "Did you ever hear of Dr. Albert Schweitzer?" Indeed they had, but that was years ago and in Africa. "Well, do you mean to tell me that there is no young doctor in America who wants to sleep during the day and work at night? We will find a night doctor." That was the end of our meeting, and, sure enough, ECCO found a night doctor within a month.

Two years and many night-time office hours later, the ECCO heath center took over the large Florence Crittenden Maternity Home in the neighborhood. It became the ECCO Community Health Center. Hilda was chairperson of the ECCO health committee and reviewed every check and receipt. The governor of Ohio came to the grand opening. It was a proud moment for Hilda and the citizens of ECCO. Hilda could barely stand on her feet at the time, but she smiled like a glowing angel.

There was another noteworthy event that occurred when Hilda's astute practical sense well served the fate of ECCO. We had hired Ivanhoe Donaldson as the ECCO Executive Director. Ivanhoe was a firebrand civil rights activist for SNCC in Mississippi. Hilda distrusted his ardency. It was her good sense that ECCO's fate depended on the good will of the Columbus politicians, who played a key role in its funding.

On a trip to Columbus, I stayed at the Columbus Athletic Club as a guest of Leopold Bernhard. It was across the street from the State Capitol Building, and all of the political deals were made at the Club. Leopold had cultivated ECCO support among the leading families of Columbus who were Club members. I had asked Ivanhoe to join me for breakfast at the Club. When Ivanhoe arrived, we went into the dining room. We waited for service, but no service came. Finally, a black waiter came to the table and said, "Negroes cannot be served in the dining room." I was shocked and Ivanhoe was furious. For the sake of ECCO, Ivanhoe braced himself from this outrage. We left the Club in great anger. The story spread through the neighborhood instantly."

That evening ECCO held an emergency assembly. About 400 people attended, the issue of the evening was whether Rev. Leopold Bernard should resign from the Club. Leopold was present and said that he would abide by the decision and made no further comment. The speeches began on both sides of the issue. Many argued eloquently that this incident disgraced the civil rights movement and was an insult to those who sacrificed their lives for the movement. Hilda rose and calmly argued that ECCO was not a civil rights organization, but rather a neighborhood government, and as such it needed relationships and support from friendly powers within the city. ECCO had political enemies in power. It was continuously threatened by city officials who wanted to get their hands on ECCO's direct funding from the federal government and do away with its independence. If the Club was where the deals were made with friends in support of ECCO, Hilda said, Leopold should remain there. It amazes me to this day to recall the anguish, eloquence, and discerning calm of this deliberation. A vote was taken and Leopold was asked to maintain his membership. Was this the right decision? Maybe it was wrong in principle, but it was right in practical judgment. ECCO retained the vital civic support to fight its political battles. Hilda's sweet reason saved the day. A public scandal may have avenged neighborhood anger, but it would have lost essential support. Downtown political friends would rally to defend their downtown Club. It was more important to their lives and habits than the destiny of ECCO. Hilda understood that after a flurry of pride, ECCO would be wasted.

Politics: Bill Clinton

In 1985, I received a call from Brian Lunde, Executive Director of the Democratic National Committee (DNC), requesting a meeting. He came downtown to my office, where we had a long discussion about the DNC's concerns about losing voters from its historic base. Brian was a good looking Nordic fellow from South Dakota. He had a degree in Marketing and prior business experience in sports marketing. He transitioned to political campaign marketing, and worked his way up to the top staff post at the DNC. His boss was Paul Kirk, chairman of the DNC, whose patron was Senator Edward

"Ted" Kennedy (D-MA).[1]

The DNC leadership was stunned by the magnitude of the re-election victory of President Ronald Reagan in 1984 and the vast number of registered Democrats who voted for Reagan. It all boiled down to why was the Party losing its union and working class voters?

Brian convinced Paul Kirk that it was time to fund a comprehensive marketing study of democratic voters about their attitude toward the Democratic Party: issues, communication, contributions, desirable candidate profiles, and the degree of involvement of registered democrats and large donors in the policy and affairs of the Party. Brian proposed to engage a commercial marketing firm rather than an established Democratic Party consultant or pollster. He wanted an objective commercial firm that had no personal stake in the outcome.

This was not to be a polling study, but a strategic marketing study to ascertain whether the Democratic Party was meeting the needs and wants of voters and donors, and how to better serve them, so they would not slide to Republican candidates.

Brian, a devotee of my bother Philip Kotler, the international guru of marketing, wanted Kotler Marketing Group (KMG) to do the study. Philip and I were both registered Democrats at the time, and KMG had never previously served a political client.

We settled on a study plan with focus groups, telephone surveys, in-depth interviews, and the whole gamut of market research methods which we typically used for commercial studies. Brian also wanted Philip personally involved in the analysis and for the presentation of the report to the DNC because of the weight of his reputation. We had a budget of $250,000. That was good money then – a pittance of what its cost would be today.

Phil thought it was a great project and readily agreed to participate

[1]Upon the death of Senator Edward Kennedy in August 2009, Kirk was appointed to the vacancy by Massachusetts Governor Deval Patrick, pending a special election in November 2009. Kirk, who pledged only to serve until a successor was elected, was a member of the U.S. Senate from September 25, 2009 through January 20, 2010, when Scott Brown, who prevailed in a special election, succeeded Kirk.

and to make the final presentation. He had written an article on political marketing from a theoretical perspective. He now had a chance to test his thoughts. Philip joined me and my partner at the time, Nelson Rosenbaum, to accept the project, under the auspices of Kotler Marketing Group, which was then operating within the legal framework of the Center for Responsive Governance (CRG) of which I was a 50 percent partner with Nelson. I led the project.

The DNC had never conducted a marketing study of its value to its registered voters and donors. Representative Thomas "Tip" O'Neil (D-MA) was then the Speaker of the U.S. House of Representatives, and the titular head of the Party. Tip was an Old Style Boston machine politician who coined the enduring slogan that: "All politics is local." By that he meant from the ground up, the voters, precinct captains, city political machines, mayors, political favors to downtown big wigs, friendly newspapers, unions, ward aldermen, and Thanksgiving turkeys. This is what it took to win! The Democratic Party had ruled city governments this way for a century.

Ronald Reagan's impressive victory over President James E. "Jimmy" Carter in 1980, while a setback, was not taken seriously until his overwhelming reelection in 1984 in defeating former Vice President Walter "Fritz" Mondale with a large flank of Democratic voters. A new generation of registered Democrats had emerged from the Vietnam anti-war days. They wanted McGovern, not the party machine! The Kennedy mystique was vanishing. The precincts were losing their edge to community action and reform politics. The Party's weakened position at the municipal level took the congressional leadership by surprise. Tip O'Neil and Paul Kirk, were scared enough to try something new. Let's find what our Democrats want before the Republicans steal the show.

Kirk had brought in a new executive staff of young campaign Turks who were savvy in marketing, media, and grass roots fundraising. They were led by Brian and his deputy George Berger. They were eager to get beyond the entrenched inside consultants to find out what was really going on.

KMG was prepared for a large-scale project. We had the computers and staff to do the job. I was 50 at the time and had a heck of a time learning how to use these new-fangled devices. As a result, I bothered the hell out of Nelson, 10-years my junior, who was more technologically deft than I.

It was a logistical challenge to organize and handle the scheduling and information processing for our planned 36 focus groups and 3,500 telephone surveys. We designed the telephone surveys and the segment sample sizes. While the telephone surveys were outsourced, we handled the focus groups internally, as well as the survey analysis. Our staff arranged the focus groups in 12 cities with three focus groups per city. Nelson and I personally split the focus groups. We each moderated 18 groups. The project took a year to plan, conduct and present. Brian Lunde and his staff, as well as Paul Kirk attended several of my focus groups, all of which were taped and recorded.

This proved to be an arduous study task for our small company. I had to transcribe the focus groups tapes and identify and analyze major themes. Nelson did the heavy lifting on the computer analysis of the telephone survey data. We consulted with Philip for his observations. We issued preliminary findings which excited Lunde and his colleagues. It was as if we were breaking the German Enigma Code at Bletchley Park. The DNC had no systematic and scientific understanding of its own voters. Democrat politicians and their trusted advisors were relying on their personal experiences of the past rather than engaging present-day realities and trends.

The preliminary findings were disturbing. Many white middle class and union Democrats felt that the Party that they grew up with was deserting them for minorities. They did not want the social programs that the Congressional leadership was imposing. They resented what they believed to be the deterioration of public education and public safety, as well as the liberality of social welfare programs. They were recoiling from defeat in the Vietnam War and saw the Party as weakening the military and caving in to the communist countries. They felt that the Party never solicited their views and had become beholden to big business.

As this disturbing news seeped into the leadership circle Brian brought me into the "club." I was invited to attend DNC meetings and meet top leaders and big donors. I had a message that had to be presented and considered. It was a message that was not forthcoming from their inner circle or Tip O'Neill's inner circle of political consultants and pollsters. No wonder they lost so heavily to Reagan! I became close to Paul Kirk. The bearer of bad news was as important asset to him for his leverage to change the status quo.

Our findings showed that the Democratic Party had to turn from the left to the center to regain middle class and blue collar support. This was no easy task, since the DNC at that time was riddled with ethnic and Left caucuses constantly putting pressure on Democratic Congressional leaders, including the Black, Hispanic, Anti-war, Anti-nuclear, Feminist, Environmental, and Anti-poverty caucuses. You name it, and there was a caucus for it – all pulling the party apart.

The research showed that registered working and middle class Democratic voters wanted the Party to move to the center. There was no internal voice from the corporate, manufacturing, and small enterprise communities. They were left out of the picture. If the American Association of Manufacturers and the U.S. Chamber of Commerce had any influence in Party circles, it was sub-rosa – unacknowledged for fear of upsetting the unions.

This was a new period of declining manufacturing in America. Beginning in the late 1970s, U.S. manufacturers were moving production off-shore for lower costs and new markets. The big companies were becoming multi-national corporations, who, along with small businesses, were the largest generators of American jobs. The Democratic Party had no public tie to the business community. I proposed to Paul Kirk that we organize a meeting of the DNC with corporate leaders. He concurred and asked me to proceed. I talked to Dean Don Jacobs of the Kellogg School of Business to arrange and host this meeting. Don lined up 12 top corporate leaders. Here, we would be breaking new ground since there had never been a publicly acknowledged meeting of corporate leaders with the DNC. Unfortunately, following pressure from Tip O'Neill and the unions, Paul Kirk had to cancel the meeting. Don Jacobs was disappointed since he had put the prestige of the Kellogg School on the line. He was a true professional in every respect and thoroughly gracious in taking the heat for this shortsighted decision to cancel this historic event.

Brian Lunde soon connected me to the Democratic Leadership Council (DLC), which was organized after the 1984 election by Governors Chuck Robb of Virginia, Bruce Babbit of Arizona, Lawton Chiles of Florida, and Senator Sam Nunn of Georgia for the purpose of moving the Democratic Party to the Center. The DLC was directed by Al From. I met Al From with Brian Lunde and briefed him on the project's findings. Our data and analysis confirmed the purpose of the DLC. Al viewed our marketing study as a cornerstone for their DLC strategy. Coincidentally, the study's preferred presidential candidate's profile matched to a tee that of DLC member, Governor Bill Clinton of Arkansas. The Democrat voters wanted a good looking candidate from the South who was a centrist with a sense of humor and a down home style. The DLC elected Clinton as its new chairman and then proceeded to promote Clinton as its candidate for victory in 1988. Our data and analysis matched the DLC instinct.

Though the DLC had the report after it was finished, its distribution within the Party was limited and eventually suppressed. Once the report was finished, and after Phillip and I presented it to Paul Kirk and Brian Lune, his immediate staff and the entire DNC staff it was released to the state party chairs and state national committee men and women, who in effect ruled the Party. The state operatives were distressed by our findings and recommendations. All hell broke loose at the top of the Party, and the report was summarily suppressed by Tip O'Neill and his cadre. It was never released, despite the pressure from the left to do so.

My work with the DNC came to an end when Thomas Edsall of the *Washington Post* called me about a hot fact in our study that Kirk denied and Lunde affirmed. "Was Paul Kirk correct or was Brian Lunde correct?" I barely thought about the question. "Brian Lunde is correct," I told him. From the strict business point of view of a vendor, I should have declined to comment; however, my respect and gratitude for Brian superseded business protocol. That comment ended my relationship with Paul Kirk, the DNC, and any subsequent political marketing work. Brian and I have remained good friends.

The Democratic Party ignored our work and ran liberal Michael Dukakis for President in 1988. He lost badly to Reagan's successor, Vice President George Herbert Walker Bush. Following that disaster, Governor Bill Clinton began his road to the White House. He was our profile candidate and was victorious against the reelection of Vice President Bush. Our study had legs!

Statesman: Senator Mark Hatfield

How often does a politician stand in genuine awe of a people? He may flatter them, but genuine respect is a rarity. More commonly, politicians would have people stand in awe of them. This is a tale of a rare public servant, who sat with a demos of local people and was profoundly moved by the wisdom of their political deliberations.

My book, *Neighborhood Government,* was well received in 1969. It was a controversial tract calling for the breakup of cities and the devolution of municipal authority to the neighborhoods. The neighborhoods would be constitutional units of state government, and they would coordinate as federated cities. The book was acclaimed by the Left as a touchstone of participatory democracy; and by the Right and Libertarians as a decentralization of power. Liberals and planners reviled the book as a death knell of expert knowledge and institutional power - a calamity of inefficiency. It was the book of the month for book clubs on the Left and the Right, including the Libertarian Book Club.

The book found its way to Governor Ronald Reagan through Frank Cook, a Washington aide to Senator Mark Hatfield (R-OR). Hatfield, who had served as governor of Oregon, was a liberal Republican who enjoyed the cross party support of Republican and Democratic voters. Cook was a scion of the California industrial Cook family, whose leader was Charlie Cook, Frank's uncle and principal financer of the Republican Party in California.

Frank was a young and good looking man in his late 20s. He graduated from Pomona College and came to Washington for political work. He had a hearty sense of humor and an unusual perspicacity that trumped dogma and enabled him to set his sights on fresh fields of political thought and action. He read my book and met me in Washington. He was very taken by my work in neighborhood organizing and it struck a chord.

Frank accomplished three things: he arranged through his colleagues in Governor. Reagan's cabinet to host a Governor's dinner to celebrate my book at the Sutter Club in Sacramento. Ed Meese chaired that dinner; Frank personally introduced me and my book to Senator Hatfield in Washington; and, he made a large financial grant that enabled me to form the Institute for Neighborhood Studies and he joined its board. Frank liked the idea of a national Republic resting upon bedrock of local democracies.

I met with Mark Hatfield in his Senate office. He had a degree in political science. His political interest was theoretical as well as practical. He had a generous intellect and we had a heartening conversation. He listened and asked questions to test my conviction about the capacity of neighborhood people to govern their public community life. He wanted to see if Jeffersonian Ward Republics could actually work. I invited him to make a visit with me to McKees Rocks, Pennsylvania, a small town outside of Pittsburgh, where I had been organizing for the past year. Frank, Hatfield, and I traveled to Pittsburgh to visit McKees Rocks.

The McKees Rocks Community Organization (MRCO) was a member of my larger organization, the National Association of Neighborhoods. MRCO was spearheaded by a young nun and priest who had gone to bat for the town's people against the mayor and his entrenched cronies. Time and again our organizing efforts to established neighborhood social, cultural, and economic development were stymied by his clique, who held the town in the palm of their hands.

One year of my organizing efforts, under the auspices of the local Catholic Church, produced strong leadership and a strong decision making assembly of residents. I was able to gain direct funding to MRCO from the U.S. Office of Economic Opportunities (OEO) and the Department of Housing and Urban Development (HUD). We received enough direct funding to run a community center, a health center, a senior citizens program, and a housing rehab program. All of these resources bypassed the mayor, which was difficult in that period, because by 1969 Community Action funds, which were originally legislated to go directly to neighborhood organizations, were now mandated to flow to city mayors who distributed this money to their cronies.

When we arrived in McKees Rocks, Senator Hatfield and Frank were heartedly received. Hatfield spent his day meeting with the people in their committees as they were deliberating their program affairs. He saw the fruit of direct federal funding to neighborhood organizations in housing rehabilitation, job training and placement, health care, and the buzz of citizen energy invested in neighborhood wellbeing. He witnessed local liberty in action. He observed the deliberative proceedings of the neighborhood assembly and saw direct democracy at work. Many national politicians visit local communities for electoral speeches and fundraising. Here was an Oregon Senator spending two days, thousands of miles from his constituency, to learn something about democratic self-government.

That night, Hatfield addressed a large public meeting of McKees Rocks citizens that was covered by the Pittsburgh TV stations. He cheered the people and the people cheered him. They were proud that a U.S. Senator from a distant state was recognizing their local achievements and spreading the message to all communities.

After the speech the chairman of the MRCO elected council asked the Senator to visit the town's Catholic parish priest. We walked to the rectory and the chairman knocked on the door. It was 9 p.m. After a short delay, the housekeeper came to the door. The chairman explained with great pride that a U.S. Senator wished to pay a brief courtesy call upon the parish priest. Instead of inviting us in, she closed the door. Six of us waited on the front door step. Ten minutes passed until she opened the door and said that the Father regrets that it is too late in the evening and was not able to see the senator.

This insouciance deflated the spirit of the McKees Rocks leaders, but Hatfield took this dismissal with a polite smile and consoled the leaders. He reminded them that "all politics is local" and that the priest probably had more to lose in soiling his relationship with a hostile mayor than any gain from welcoming a distant Senator.

Hatfield, Frank and I traveled back to Washington with a powerful shared experience. Hatfield and I forged a common bond that lasted several years. Hatfield told me that the visit to McKees Rocks was the most satisfying political experience of his life.

The following year, Hatfield introduced in the Senate several remarkable pieces of legislation supporting the establishment of neighborhood governments. One bill proposed to federally charter neighborhood governments. Another bill altered the federal income tax code to direct federal income tax payments directly to neighborhood level governments to retain their allocation and remit the balance to the federal government.

We promoted this legislation at the 1972 Republican Convention in Miami by placing printed copies on every delegate's seat in the convention hall. Leopold Bernhard and I joined Frank Cook at the convention. Hatfield did not attend because his progressive Oregon politics got him as many Democrat as Republican votes. Frank sponsored a reception in support of the proposed legislation in a hall that could accommodate a hundred people. One lady showed up.

The cruelest blow came from George Will, a former writer for the *National Review* and a new columnist for the *Washington Post*. Will lampooned the Hatfield legislation as a constitutional travesty and absurd political program. This was his inaugural column for the *Post* and the death knell of a Congressional strategy for neighborhood government.

I had two edifying experiences at that Republican convention. In the first case, Frank invited us to his Uncle Charlie Cook's hotel room to meet this Nixon power broker. When we got off the elevator there was a line of perhaps 30 people waiting to pay homage to Mr. Cook. We walked past the line directly into the room. Cook met Leopold and me with bland indifference. Leopold's clerical collar broke no ice. We spoke to Charlie for five minutes about neighborhoods. He said nothing until his impatience broke forth and he called to his wife, "Helen, did you bring the Cheesettes?" His wife went through two suitcases to retrieve a box of Cheesettes and other snack food. This old skinflint would not think of spending an extra dime in Miami.

The high point of the convention was the anti-war protest outside the Miami convention hall. A thousand protesters lined the streets and chanted blaring rebukes to the delegates. "Stop the War," rang out like peeling church bells. The Miami police broke up the protest and arrested a pack of protesters, including my friend Rennie Davis of Students for a Democratic Society (SDS). Shortly afterwards, I got a call in my hotel room from a friend on the Left who was at the protest. "Milton, can you put your hands on $2,000 to post bail for Rennie?" Since I didn't have any money I called Frank Cook for the cash. Frank gave me the cash in an hour. Rennie was released. Nothing was said to Charlie Cook. He would have blown his stack!

Frank's wholesome politics finally got the ire of Uncle Charlie. Just as Charlie had sabotaged Frank's father from Cook Enterprises, he now broke Frank. Frank was tossed out of the family enterprise and fortune. He left Hatfield to find his own independent way. We kept in touch for years through Frank's travails until we finally lost track. Hatfield died, leaving behind the Jeffersonian legacy of neighborhood legislation. To my knowledge no scholar has ever reviewed this bequest to democracy.

We live today in an elite republic. Hatfield saw something new. Things are changing. As the world turns, local liberty may rise again, and we may be able to rest our national Republic on a bedrock of constitutional neighborhood democracies.

Dignity: U.S. Rep. Henry Gonzalez

Did you ever see a sitting member of the U.S. Congress cry? I did, and it broke my heart. Men of power are thought to be invulnerable to personal offense. Political and monetary power is a personal salve. It is the little guys, especially minority little guys, who are thought to be victims of indignity.

Honor is a universal feeling, and dishonor is a universal moral breach. Those at the top suffer dishonor as much as those at the bottom. It is an intellectual error to subscribe to hierarchies of human need. A poor man suffers the want of material sustenance for himself and his family; but he has no less a sense of his human worth than a rich man. He can suffer moral indignity no less harshly than material want. Similarly, no amount of riches can secure a rich man or woman's confidence against debasement by their peers. This is precisely what happened to Congressman Henry Gonzalez (D-TX), and caused him to weep in my presence.

Henry Gonzalez, now deceased, was a rugged and independent Congressman who represented his district in San Antonio, Texas, for 17 terms. His ancestors came from Europe to Mexico in 1561, and thrived as wealthy ranchers and miners until the Mexican revolution of 1910. His family fled to San Antonio where he was born in 1916. His forbears had made their Mexican fortune in the region of San Antonio when it was part of Mexico.

Gonzalez became an attorney and politician in San Antonio until he ascended to the U.S. House of Representatives in 1961, where he served for many years on the subcommittee on Housing and Community Development of the House Banking Committee. He fought to ensure affordable housing for the poor and elderly. He was a staunch supporter of the Community Reinvestment Act which aimed to reduce discriminatory credit practices against low-income neighborhoods, a practice known as redlining.

Henry was a tough looking guy. His face was raw as putty, with overlapping wrinkles and folds. His nose was large and definitive. His mouth was broad and assertive. His brows were the platform of quizzical eyes. It was a face that you would not want to mess with if you were a foe; but a face that embraced and protected his family and friends.

According to the *New York Times*, *"Mr. Gonzalez is universally regarded as a stormy-tempered, fiercely unabashed populist, beholden to no one and disinclined to issue apologies."* While this characterization is true of his attitude to enemies, it was not true of his behavior to friends.

As the founder and CEO of the National Associations of Neighborhoods in the 1970s, I was a leader in a broad coalition of urban neighborhood organizations. We had many meetings with Rep. Gonzalez because much of our agenda fell under the purview of his subcommittee. He was a proponent of our interests and views, and a staunch advocate in our struggle for the Community Reinvestment Act. The legislation finally passed in 1977. At a Congressional hearing on the bill, I was upbraided during my testimony by Democratic Rep. Fernand St. Germain (D-RI).

"Mr. Kotler, you are saying that neighborhood organizations should regulate our banks. That is Communism."

"Respectfully", I submitted, "It is democracy. If the federal, state, and local government can regulate banks, why can't the neighborhoods in which they are operating regulate them?"

"Neighborhoods are not governments!"

"Congressman St. Germain, that is precisely our aspiration, and Senator Hatfield has introduced neighborhood government legislation to that effect."

Rep. Gonzalez interrupted St. Germain, "There you go again with Communism. Every time someone raises an idea that you object to, you call them Communists. I've been called a Communist plenty of times, and I say phooey!" Gonzalez got me off the hook in his typical blunt manner. Our friendship deepened. Gonzalez was a consistent and vigorously supporter of many things that NAN strove to achieve legislatively.

One day in 1981, I received a call from my friend Richard Kaufman, who was Director of the Joint Economic Committee and who had been a legislative director for Rep. Gonzalez for a decade. Richard was very fond of Gonzalez.

"Milton, I am asking you for a favor."

What's up, Richard!

"Henry Gonzalez is in great distress and very depressed. Henry Reuss (D-WI) has stepped down and Henry is next in line by seniority for chairing the subcommittee on Housing and Community development. The trouble is that his Democratic peers don't want him to chair the subcommittee.

"What's the problem?"

"They think he is wild, and it boils down to the fact he won't take money from banking or housing lobbyists and they don't want a Spic to chair the subcommittee. "

"What do you want me to do?"

"He needs to know that community people need him and love him. He needs the will to fight for his right. Can you talk to him?"

I scheduled an appointment with Gonzalez. When we met in his office, he was drawn and blue. He welcomed me in a sad and depressed mood. His head lay cupped in his hands on his desk.

"Milton, they don't want me. They don't respect me. I've given twenty years to this committee and the god dam gringos don't want me."

There he was in his polyester suit sitting at his desk, a man who never postured to the high life of Washington, and who went home every weekend to his family and constituents in Texas. He shrugged his shoulders and looked at me as a friend with whom he could share his disconsolate feelings. I put my hands on his broad shoulders with genuine affection.

He began to weep. "I'm not going to fight them. I've been on the committee longer than any of them. I know how it works and the good that it can do for ordinary people. My own party doesn't want my leadership to help people. They are only for the big shots."

I was saddened to see this tough guy browbeaten and despondent.

"Mr. Gonzalez, don't give up. We need you. If you don't stand up and fight for what is rightfully yours by House rules of seniority, how can communities stand up and fight for their needs? For us, it is a battle of power. For you it is a matter of right. If you cave in, we don't stand a chance."

He looked up at me with a transformed gesture of resolve. No more tears and a bold smile, I'll fight those bastards." I rejoined, "We will fight for you. " We did. The Neighborhood Coalition and NAN organized actions in the Congressional districts of his Democrat enemies on the subcommittee. We publicized and protested their opposition to our defender Gonzalez. It was a rebellion of Democrat voters against their Democrat representatives in the House to support Henry Gonzalez, or else!

Henry pulled all of his strings with the Democrat House leadership. This one-two punch of bottom up and top down tactics was too much for Henry's opponents. They capitulated and Henry won and became chairman of the Subcommittee on Housing and Community Development of the House Banking Committee for the 97th Congress in 1981, and later became Chairman of the House Banking Committee in 1989 through 1995. What an organizing victory!

In February, 1981, NAN sponsored a victory party for Henry

Gonzalez in the House Banking Committee hearing room. We had a big turnout and Henry gave a great speech. Its highlight was his remark that his political peers underestimated his political skill.

"My nasty colleagues underestimated me. They disparaged me because of my ethnic heritage. They did not understand the heritage of my political skill. My forbears were mayors of San Antonio and other Mexican cities for two centuries before the Mexican-American war of 1835. Texas was lost to the United States, but the centuries of the Gonzalez family political skills were never lost. With your help, I outsmarted the snobs. " Applause!

Henry invited me to the House dining room for lunch a month later. "Milton thanks for the confidence you gave me when I hit rock bottom, and thank your people. Is there anything that I can do for you?" "No," I responded, "Just keep fighting for the little guys."

Glory: Ivanhoe Donaldson

The paradox of equal rights is that it takes political power to achieve this aim. Political power is cunning. It plays the trick of achieving collective gain at a cost of the personal corruption of many of its leaders, who engorge the fruit of victory along the way. The civil rights movement has deservedly succeeded through the struggle of black power, but it has left a waste of corrupt appetite in its wake.

Several hundred celebrants gathered at the Metropolitan A.M.E. on M street in Washington D.C. on May 13, 2016 to memorialize the passing of a great civil rights warrior Ivanhoe Donaldson.

Ivanhoe is worthy of praise. He was a brave leader of SNCC in both Alabama and Mississippi, and rallied the troops on Selma. He was a man of action and a trainer of men of action. He deserves glory; but we must understand a thing about glory.

Glory is more of a benefice for those who glorify a leader than for the glorified leader. The gloried are dead with all of their secrets and ambivalences. The private interstices of the life of heroes never enter the legend. These are the clumsy details of personal existence that confuse the broad brush of valiancy – corrupting circumstances that muffle the mighty descant of triumph. Their only value is to cast a shadow on blinding fame, and enable us to talk about the person, rather than celebrate ourselves.

This tale is about parts of Ivanhoe's life that are not mentioned in his eulogies. It is not that Ivanhoe erased these episodes for shame or irrelevance. They undoubtedly had had some unknown personal value for him. It is simply a side of his life about which his celebrants could make no sense of him or for themselves. This is material for the story teller, not the myth maker.

Ivanhoe Donaldson was a handsome tawny figure whom I hired in 1967 as Organizer for the East Central Citizens Organization (ECCO), Columbus, Ohio) in 1967; then brought to the Institute for Policy Studies (IPS) in Washington DC as a Fellow to work with me on neighborhood government. He soon lost interest as my partner in neighborhood empowerment, and decided to use his time at IPS to go after the big fish of organizing city mayoral campaigns for prominent black community figures. He organized Marion Berry's mayoral victory in Washington, D.C. and successful campaigns in other cities with large black populations. Ivanhoe left IPS for several corporate jobs with high salaries; and eventually became Deputy Mayor of Washington, DC under Mayor Marion Barry, where he engineered hid mix of good deeds and real estate deals for local developers. That job ended when he was convicted of embezzling $190,000 of D.C. public funds. He spent three years in jail. After his release, he was back on the street with all of his contacts working again with developers and making lots of money.

My first knowledge of Ivanhoe was in Washington DC in 1966 at a meeting with Bob Moses and Marc Raskin, leader of IPS. I had asked Marc to introduce me to Bob Moses, then head of SNCC's Mississippi project, to get a recommendation for an organizer to come to ECCO.

ECCO (East Central Citizens Organization) was a black neighborhood of 5,000 residents and roughly one square mile in Columbus, Ohio. We needed a full time Organizer to replace my periodic visits to Columbus from Washington DC. This was a federal funded neighborhood government project which I first organized with Leopold Bernhard in 1964 to transfer a white

Lutheran Church school and social center building and its funded programs to the neighborhood control of ECCO. Matters were getting too complicated for me and Pastor Bernhard and his church staff and neighborhood leaders to handle. We needed a full time organizer. Bob Moses heard my story, was interested in the model of neighborhood government, and recommended that I meet Ivanhoe Donaldson.

Ivanhoe came to meet me in Washington. We exchanged backgrounds and I oriented him to the project and its leadership. He took the assignment and planned to drive from Mississippi to Columbus in a month to after settling some matters in Mississippi. I had a month to travel to Columbus, discuss his assignment with neighborhood and church leaders, and prepare a residence for him.

Anticipating Ivanhoe's arrival, I travelled to Columbus to welcome him. He would inform me when he arrived. I was with Leopold and Thelma Bernhard when we got a call from Ivanhoe. He was arrested for vagrancy and attempted assault on an officer as soon as he crossed into the border of the Columbus municipality. He asked us to come to the police station and spring him.

I joined Leopold at the police station. Leopold asked the Duty Officer to see Ivanhoe. The Officer claimed that Ivanhoe ran a red light, violated parking regulations and abused an Officer; and declined our request to see him. Leopold mustered his Teutonic clerical authority and threatened to bring charges unless we saw Ivanhoe. The strength of Leopold's robust spirit and clerical muster carried the issue and Ivanhoe appeared.

Ivanhoe claimed that the FBI had tracked his travel from Mississippi and informed the Columbus police to book him, - that he was up to no good! The police said nothing and released Ivanhoe to Leopold's custody.

Ivanhoe remained in Columbus for six months and improved our administration of programs and community promotion of ECCO. The leadership of the community accepted him because Leopold and I backed him. Several key leaders like Hilda Ellison and Rufus Linville were apprehensive that his SNCC militancy was not appropriate for ECCO's purpose.

The tension between them rested on real disagreement. For

Hilda, ECCO was a Neighborhood Government, not a Civil Rights organization. Neighborhood Government to Hilda and other leaders meant direct community governance of the social and economic programs funded directly to ECCO by the Federal Government for job training and placement, neighborhood health care, housing assistance; culture and arts, literacy, nutrition, and many other community needs. All of these federally supported programs required political and business support to sustain the direct flow of funds to ECCO, rather than through the city government. ECCO needed good will to fulfill the purpose of neighborhood self-government.

To Hilda and other key community leaders, the Civil Rights movement was a vital struggle for political rights and dignity. The Civil Rights Movement was about equal political rights, not neighborhood self-government. She supported the Civil Rights Movement as a Black citizen of the United States, but ECCO was set up for another purpose – neighborhood self-government. She wanted ECCO to improve the lives of 5,000 people in the ECCO community. This is issue of conflicting views came to a head within three months of Ivanhoe's tenure.

Leopold was a member of the Columbus Athletic Club, across the street from the Ohio State Capitol. It was the key political and social club in town. Trent Sickles, represented the Lazurus interests (Federated Stores, later to become Macy's, Bloomingdale, etc.). He was a friend of Leopold's and very helpful politically to ECCO. Other leading families included the Wolfs and Galbraith (Nationwide Insurance)...and so it went. This is where the business and political deals were made and Leopold made it a point to have hi church and ECCO connected to this the inner circle local power. I occasionally stayed at the Club as a guest of Leopold.

On one trip I planned to stay at the Club and arranged with Ivanhoe to join me there for breakfast. I arrived the night before and went down to the dining room for an 8AM breakfast with Ivanhoe. I arrived before him and was seated at a table. Ivanhoe arrived and joined me at the table. We waited for the waiter for a long time, until finally a Negro waiter came to the table and asked Ivanhoe to please leave because Blacks were not served in the ginning room. Ivanhoe was stunned and irate – 1967 and no Blacks allowed. This was Columbus, Ohio, not Mississippi! I asked for the manger to explain this insult, He assured me that it was club policy. Ivanhoe got up in a heat and I followed. We left the room and I checked out of the club.

We informed Leopold and the ECCO leaders of this episode and an ECCO assembly was called for the next evening. About three hundred neighbors packed the Church. Leopold left the matter his membership entirely up to the community's deliberative decision. If they wanted him to resign, after deliberating about the matter, he would do so without hesitation. If not, he would continue his membership. He agreed to answer questions of fact, but declined to express his opinion on the matter or his advice. Upon questioning, he described the Club and its powerful members, and the deals made there that affected the City and the ECCO neighborhood.

People argued reasonably and passionately against the bigoted Club. Many declaimed that insult was egregious and that Leopold should resign. Others argued for his continued membership to help ECCO's self-governing interests. After two hours of debate, a vote was taken. The motion to resign from the club was defeated. This was a remarkable decision for a Black assembly of hundreds of adults, unparalleled at the time for political prudence, and a complete mystery to me to this day. Somehow, neighborhood government took root as it never did before and has never done since.

Ivanhoe could never accept this decision. For him, neighborhood government was an experimental method for civil rights agitation and strategy. For ECCO civil right was a sister of local liberty. Ivanhoe may have taken this as a lack of confidence in his leadership. He left ECCO shortly afterwards.

I had great respect for Ivanhoe's intellect and brave action. I invited him to IPS and - arranged with Marc to receive him as a visiting fellow. Ivanhoe came.

My intellectual break with Ivanhoe came within six months at IPS. I had been doing some organizing in the Adams Morgan neighborhood of Washington, DC, as well as in Boston, Chicago, and Buffalo, NY. I was eager to do another Neighborhood Government project with him.

He kindly and emphatically informed me that he was no longer interested in community organization and had set his eyes on getting black community leaders elected to city government. From that time forward, Ivanhoe built his relations with young black leaders in DC like Marion Barry, Stokeley Carmichael, Cortland Cox, Charlie Cobb, and others. He compiled a list of viable black mayoral candidates around the country. He won the support of Marc Raskin, and I supported this, mindful of its gain to equal rights but loss to community self-governance. Elective city politics was not my cup of tea.

This was the beginning of Ivanhoe's career as a prominent national dealmaker among black politicians. The Neighborhood movement lost a brilliant player. Black politicians gained a brilliant political strategist.

After Marion Barry's Mayoral victory under the brilliant baton of Ivanhoe's campaign organization and management, he appointed Ivanhoe as Deputy Mayor. Ivanhoe never asked for my advice on any urban matter. He delivered deals with for Washington real estate moguls, and made lots of money. To his credit, Ivanhoe's deals advanced affordable housing for poor folks and the elderly.

Ivanhoe became rich. One evening Topper Care and I were walking on Connecticut Avenue and passed Dupont Liquor. Ivanhoe was inside at the counter with five bottles of expensive wine and two dozen long stem red roses. Topper and I offered to help him carry his bounty his car. He welcomed our help and we walked to his car. It was a Mercedes sports car. He had to lower the front seat back to fit the roses without bending the stems. We put the wine in the trunk. He thanked us and went off to his good life.

During the early 1980s I would see Ivanhoe nattily dressed on Connecticut Avenue near Duke Zeiberts below Dupont Circle. He would ask how and what I was doing...and that I should lose weight...and always concluding, "Let's get together". In 1986 he was indicted and convicted of embezzling $190,000 of City money and sentenced to seven years in jail. It was a careless transparent theft...no clever laundering. He was released after serving three years.

I saw him several times after release. He was back on the street helping real estate developers get zoning permissions and tax rebates to open new parts of the city for redevelopment. His friends were still in place in the city bureaucracy and money flowed. He also played in national politics as a fundraiser and strategist for Jesse Jackson and black mayors who had their eye on Congress. His crime made no waves. He moved back into the IPS as a Fellow once again. Marc Raskin extended a generous hand to Ivanhoe. Ivanhoe needed the cover and wider political scope of the Institute. Whenever I saw him he insisted that we should get together. I always concurred, but nothing came of it.

What are we to make of this brilliant fellow, who braved a path for civil rights, carried black community leaders into elective office, and dipped his hand in the till along the way? It is not enough to dismiss his criminal conviction as the bad luck of getting caught. Ivanhoe did not have the intent or spirit of a criminal. He sought power for a great purpose of equal rights. But, like many of his ambitious peers, he never had a heritage of power to realize and withstand the corrupting nature of power. To an ingénue, power begins as a noble purpose and ends as corrupt enrichment. If caught, the outcome is scrubbed, so long as new deals can continue, more cash to spread around to advance the career of colleagues, and some social good done along the way. The legend is not tarnished.

High Spirit: Barbara Raskin

"As Vivacity is the Gift of Women, Gravity is that of Men."

Joseph Addison

Barbara Bellman Raskin died in 1999 at the age of 63. Her memorial service was held at the Quaker House in Washington, D.C. The meeting hall was packed with devoted friends, family, and feminist camp followers. Eulogists were numerous, including remarks by Christopher Hitchens and Betty Frieden that heralded Barbara's literary prowess and feminism. Greta and I were solemnly present. Barbara's former husband, Marc Raskin, concluded the program with a touching piano performance of Debussy's "Claire de Lune." The event was a rare blend of Barbara's vivacity and Marc' gravity – a contest that dogged and foiled their married life.

Barbara wrote five novels. *Hot Flashes* was a *New York Times* best seller for 20 weeks. But her more astonishing novel was her first book, *Loose Ends*, which scandalized her domestic married life in 1960s left-wing Washington, and may have paved the way for her eventual divorce from Marc. She followed that marriage with the discovery that marriage was no longer de rigueur. So began a burgeoning feminist literary career. Barbara's literary strength was her outrageous wit and the courage to satirize herself in the domestic and political landscape of male importunities. Her circle of wives, girlfriends, and readers railed as she cudgeled male domination.

Barbara was an attractive Jewish gal from Minnesota. She was of medium height, well figured and swarthy. Her skin was smooth as silk, and her calves were firm and svelte. Her black hair was fulsome and her dark eyes arrested attention. Her pretty face was benign in calm circumstance, but inflamed when passionate. She had a humorous and excitable nature.

Marc, Barbara and I, along with my roommate Roy Sanders, were good chums at the University of Chicago. Barbie, as we called Barbara, and Marc were dating for a year. She was impatient for marriage. Though he vouchsafed his love, he resisted a dénouement. One night we gave Marc a Mickey Fin, bound him in a rope and laid him flat on the back floor of my car. Barbie was so excited that she peed in her pants. We drove to Indiana to find a Justice of the Peace to tie the hymeneal knot. Barbie was a comic Juliet. The only problem was that we had to wake up Marc for the event. Even in Indiana, Justices of the Peace would not marry zombies. When Marc woke he screamed for freedom and, like Samson, tore loose from his tethers. The joke was over and we returned to Chicago – a god laugh and no harm done.

Barbie was passionate about writing. In 1957, there was a $500 Ida Noyes prize for the best short story by a male student. Barbie had a story and wanted the confidence of a prize and its bag of money. She convinced Roy, who loved her, to submit the story under his name. Hosanna, he won! Roy, who had never written a fictive word in his life, was suddenly a literary giant on campus. He wasted the rest of term bootlessly scribbling words to warrant his stature, while Marc and Barbie married and went off to Italy to spend her honorarium.

Marc, who had completed law School, advanced his piano studies and Barbie wrote stories, until it was time to for them to return to the U.S. and move to Washington, D. C., for a Congressional staff job. That move was the beginning of Marc's political adventures. He spent several years as legislative counsel to Democrat Rep. Sidney Yates of Chicago, and then graduated to become a White House assistant to Mc George Bundy, National Security Advisor to President John F. Kennedy. After several years, he organized the Institute for Policy Studies (IPS) and commenced a brilliant career of political thought and action.

I frequently visited Marc and Barbie in Washington, while I remained at the University of Chicago. They beseeched me come and join them at IPS. In 1963, I capitulated began a 14 year stint at IPS.

While Marc tilled the political soil of Washington, Barbie raised three children, ran a house of visiting dissidents, and continued to write. As Marc toiled with political change, Barbie boiled with literary frustration, tedious mothering, and frustrated romance. Both began to lead secret lives. Marc's secret romance culminated in their separation; while Barbie's secret life seeded the imagination and energy of her first novel, *Loose Ends*, which parodied her married life with ribald energy.

Barbie turned to feminist writing as her raison d'être. Her feminist novels paralleled Marc's puissant pursuit of radical politics. Her later novels became didactic and tendentious. She lost the hilarious foil of Marc's cuckolded domesticity. As she rose in feminist politics, her literary quality deteriorated. Barbie was a comedian and did not wear grave concerns well. She was a master of satire, now barren of source, and a tepid protagonist of a cause for which she essentially had no heart.

I knew Barbie very well. We were funny together. I sweetened her torpid moods. She trusted me and shared her deepest secrets. She always needed a man, because she was an incorrigible romantic. Feminism was sound in principle for Barbie, but no substitute for earthen passion. She needed what she never got from a man – adoration. She wanted to be consummately loved, but her mind was too mercurial to sustain a man's devotion.

Ambition for success disturbed her focus. She married Marc because she knew he was going places. At the time she was naive to suppose that abiding romance would follow suit. Marc wanted success only. Ambition was his fulcrum. Unlike Barbie, he was never confounded by the wry mix of ambition and romance.

Barbie had the worst possible marriage. She married a man as desirous of adoration as she was. They both fought doggedly for adoration, each in their own and separate way. He won adoration in political life, which lasted his entire life. She failed to gain devoted adoration in romantic life. She won a degree of social and literary recognition, but never the height of Marc's triumph. This piqued her body and soul and she died of a cancer that tore her veins. Marc, who never vested in romantic devotion to a woman, lived for another 20 years in devotion to a political cause that was less winsome than a woman's heart.

Musical Devotion: Ben Rosen

I deeply miss my violin buddy, Ben Rosen, who was my vivid friend from the late early1980s until his death, at 104 in 1999. Ben was a violinist and owned a music shop in LA. I was in Washington, D.C., and an avid collector of violin short piece scores. I also travelled frequently to Los Angeles for business. We were introduced to each other through George at Dale Music on Georgia Avenue in DC. Dale Music was the incomparable emporium of music material for Washington – scores, instruments, and supplies until it closed its doors on June 30, 2014, after 64 years of service to the Washington musical community.

George knew of my collecting interest. "There's a guy who you should meet. He lives in Los Angeles (LA) and has the largest collection of violin scores that I know of. He used to come to our store with steamer trunks of pirated Russian scores. He'd look through our old stuff. Here's his phone number."

I called Ben to introduce myself. He invited me to visit him in LA, which I did on my next trip, meeting him at his shop on Wilshire Boulevard. Ben was a wisp of an octogenarian who sat in a swivel chair in front of his floor-to-ceiling and wall-to-wall shelves of music scores. The scores were predominantly out-of- print treasures, bundled alphabetically by composer. There were a few shelves of new commercial scores of studies and familiar short pieces, labeled Globe Music Publications. It was really a musical score antique shop.

At the time, Ben was then 87 and weighed no more than 110 pounds. He had a classic Yiddish face with horn rimmed glass that balanced a balding scalp with a still handsome nose and once fulsome lips. (Think of George Burns without his hairpiece.) His determined chin rested upon the shriveled neck of an old man. He wore a dress shirt and tie that could no longer closely bind his collar to his neck; and a well-worn sport jacket.

"Welcome, Milton. Look around." I was dazzled by the vastness and obscurity of his collection. I knew Sarasate's *Zigeunerweisen*, but had never seen or heard his Introduction *and Terantelle, Zortzico de Iparraguire, Seranata Anduluza, Jota Aragonesa,* and 40 other Sarasate short violin pieces in 19th century florid editions. The collection swept from well-known to forgotten composers. It was like entering a stalactite cave of gorgeous crystalline forms. This was a galaxy of virtuosic violin and chamber music that overwhelmed my own mere asteroid collection.

He had a few bins of editions for sale which I ruffled through and selected for purchase. The price of the pieces ranged from $2.50 to $10.00. I bought 20 selections.

"Ben, it is an honor to meet you. How did you amass this magnificent collection?"

"It is a long story. To make it short, I did it because no one else did it. As a violinist I loved the short pieces for their characteristic quality and virtuosic composition. When I was young, violinists thrilled audiences with these pieces. They were knuckle busters and separated the wheat from the chaff among performers. Audiences howled at a precocious performance of Ernst's Last Rose of Summer. They wept and cheered Hubay's *Hejre Kati*. These pieces touched the heart. So I am a curator of the violin heart. And you, Milton, why do your search for these pieces?"

"Their sentiment," I sheepishly replied because I myself could not play many of these pieces with the perfection they deserved. I felt for their charm.

"Let's play some duets together to stretch your playing," he kindly proffered. So we began a friendship that lasted for 20 years.

Ben closed the shop and we walked to his apartment two blocks away. We stopped at a bakery for day old rye bread. "It's cheaper and also better for your health than fresh rye bread. The rye seeds have to lose some of their fat." This was the first of many dietary prescriptions that Ben advanced over the years. He stewed dried fruit into compote for breakfast. He ate boiled and jarred chicken, carrots and celery for lunch. His biggest warning was against horseradish. I would regularly order gefilte fish at the neighborhood deli. With too much of a dab of horseradish, I would sneeze. "Why are you eating horseradish when your body is rejecting it?" I had no good answer.

Ben maintained his one-bedroom apartment, so it had a dusty and comfortable veneer. The place was strewn with music. We went to an early dinner at his favorite all-you-can-eat Korean restaurant. After dinner we returned to his apartment and played Mozart and Spohr duos. Afterwards, he read me some of his own composed Yiddish poetry. I said goodnight and drove to my cottage at the famed Ambassador Hotel.

I spent the next day with him and many days on subsequent visits, rummaging through his collection. Ben did not sell his prize solos and chamber music. He rented them out to performers for a pittance. He told me stories about Heifetz, Elman, Milstein, and Kriesler all coming to him for obscure scores. Many of Europe's great musical composers, conductors, and performers like Stravinsky, Goldmark, Waxman, Milhaud, Schoenberg, and Heifetz settled in LA as refugees before World War ll (WW II). The movie industry gave them employment and they produced fabled movie music.

Jascha Heifetz frequented Ben's shop for rare short pieces. He once asked Ben for Hubay's *Echo des Alpes*. Ben has an 1894 copy and offered it to Heifetz for $5 dollars. Heifetz objected, "You last sold me his *Morceaux* for $2.50." Heifetz' silver Bentley did not deter him from penny pinching.

Ben had some money. It did not come from his shop. During one two-day visit, aside from me, only one customer came to the shop, a young girl who wanted a Sevcik study book. "Opus 8 or Opus 9," Ben queried. "I don't know," the young girl replied. "Go to your teacher and ask which opus." So Ben foreswore the only sales opportunity of the day.

Ben's money had come to him as a pirate. After WW II, he went to Europe and bought large stocks of Leipzig, East Germany, scores for a pittance. Then he went to Russia, which also had no international copyright agreement, and did the same. He filled his steamer trunks with entire publisher lists of violin, chamber music, piano and orchestra scores. Returning to the U.S., he printed and peddled these scores as Globe Music Publishers, never paying a penny of royalty. He undercut the Schirmer catalog by 50 percent and built his nest egg – the nest egg supporting his modest life style for 40 years. The shop was only a way to indulge his hobby and spend his days.

Over the next 10 years, I made frequent visits to LA for business matters and to see Ben, investigate his collection, and play music together. Ben gave me the key to his apartment and welcomed me to stay with him whenever I wished. I would call him from Washington to see how his old frame was withstanding the ravishes of time. Ben was passing through his 90s and still holding fort at Globe Music. I would ask him, "Ben, how are you doing?" His response would be, "It's 10:30 in the morning, and I'm still alive."

Sherry Kloss, Heifetz' master class assistant at UCLA, organized a 100th birthday party for Ben. I flew in for the great occasion. A grand pack of violinists attended including Rostand. Each of them owed a momentous debt to Ben for his short pieces which they played and recorded. Ben's collection was a vital link of sustaining a tradition of virtuosic violin performance that had asted for three centuries.

I subsequently engaged Sherry for two performances in Washington. She as a smash hit with Jewish violin music at Temple Sinai and rose to glory performing the Holdridge *Violin Concerto* with the Washington Symphony Orchestra. I also arranged an interview for Sherry with Susan Stanberg of National Public Radio. Sherry built a teaching and performance career as the curator of the Heifetz tradition. She has performed his short pieces all over the world with the Tononi violin that Heifetz bequeathed to her.

Sherry loved Ben as a musical treasure. Ben knew the short piece violin literature better than any violinist, including Heifetz. She tells the story of Heifetz's search for a short piece. "Heifetz", she recounted, "wanted the particular piece for a performance. He could not recall the name of the piece or the composer; only the melody. He called Ben and hummed the melody. Ben instantly named the piece, the composer, and provided the score."

In the last decade of Ben's life his home management became a serious issue, Ben engaged a strange fellow, Lynn Etcetera, as his home aide. Lynn was a Pulcinella figure. He looked like a rooster and acted like a rooster; and, like a rooster, he protected his hen, Ben.

I visited Ben several times in his last years. He had closed his store and passed his stock on to dutiful fiends in Pasadena, who had diligently cared for him for three decades. They have his collection, or what remains of it after Lynn ripped off his tithe. Ben's sister, who lived in New York, called me after his death. She was going through his effects and was disturbed that his Yiddish poetry was missing. I had met her at Ben's 100th birthday party and consoled her for her loss of Ben's beautiful poetry.

Little did she know of Ben's extravagance at the age of 90 to endow a Russian girlfriend with a home in Riverside, California. "Why did you give her a $200,000 home," I asked. "She blew my dick." Old men will go to great lengths to stay alive.

Blithe Spirit: Julian Knox

Julian Knox lived among the happy gods. He embodied the spirit of Thalia, the Goddess of merriment and festivity, and brought cheer to my sad home after the divorce and separation of my young sons from my bosom.

Julian was introduced to me in 1972 by Stanley Weiss, my friend and Institute for Policy Studies (IPS) patron. Stanley was the king of manganese and resided in Mexico City, Washington, D.C., and London. I had adventures with Stanley and his graceful and willowy wife, Lisa, in Mexico. We became familiar with each other's personality and moods. Stanley felt the burden of my solitude. What better way to cheer me than to introduce me to his British acquaintance, the charming Julian Knox, who had moved to Washington and was looking for place to live.

Julian Knox was a mental health advocate in London and a close friend of Hephzibah Menuhin (pianist and sister of Yehudi Menuhin) and her husband Richard Hauser, a spokesperson for liberal causes and a crusader for Kurdish liberty. Stanley met Julian through the Hausers and enjoyed his delightful company in London. He followed Julian's move to Washington, D.C., and advised him to get in touch with me.

Julian had left his Mental Health Institute in London, as well as his wife Jillian and son, to find his fortune in the halcyon locus of Washington's Kennedy and Johnson era, where ideas like mental health were newly celebrated and raised to government policy attention and salaries. Julian needed a job and American coffers were larger than UK budgets.

Julian came to my home in 1972. He lost no time in amusing me with his stories of the people he already knew in Washington, principally Georgetown, where he was temporarily bunking with the family of Ambassador Charles E, Bohlen. Things were getting a bit gnarled with the Ambassador's daughter Avis, and it was necessary for Julian to find new lodgings.

Julian articulated an upper class London speech. He and his brother had been Hungarian war orphans adopted by a childless aristocratic family in Sussex. They gave him a fine public school and university education and enough of a pedigree to hobnob around the clubs of London, picking up a stipend here and there, but no permanent position. Like many impecunious patricians, he lived on enough credit to meet the right people in London, like the Menuhins and Stanley Weiss. He eventually found his way, along with his walnut colored Rover sedan, to the promised and of Washington, D.C., and the Georgetown diplomatic community.

Julian was a cheerful looking chap on the stout side. His dress was impeccable and his manner jocose and scintillating. He was quite smart and thought it best not to trouble people with thought, when he could delight them with merriment. He had a round cherubic face of pinkish complexion at all time poised to smile. His hairline was thin and his body was energetic. He was my age in his late 30s and had enough jocosity to make him appealing.

After a few visits, we were playing violin duets and inviting friends over for a jolly sing-along guided by his artful piano playing. He was the life of the party, so long as he was fueled by wine and brandy. He had a special knack for Gypsy Czardas and enraptured his audience with a prodigious and zestful flair. We settled on a rental agreement and Julian moved in.

Julian met my friends and visited IPS. He met my girlfriend Greta, who adored his humor, musical talent, and buoyant charm. We would dine out, especially at Csisko's, a Hungarian restaurant, where Julian would cajole the gypsy fiddler to rest for a moment and lend him his instrument. He would brighten like a poppy and caper from table to table with Magyar ditties and romances. Julian had the verve to roast a suckling pig for our Thanksgiving feast.

As the weeks moved on, Julian spent less time cavorting with me and my friends and drifted off to Georgetown, where he played poker with the Joseph Alsop crowd of Ben Bradley, Ambassador Bohlen, and other notable diplomats and journalists. He never invited me to join those excursions. He would come home late, tipsy and broke.

He occasionally brought girlfriends to the house, like Lucy Riesman, the daughter of David Riesman, and other well-heeled ladies from whom he borrowed money. He would spend his daytime hours in the house writing job proposals, calling people for money, drinking wine, arranging his calendar, and just piddling around like a rusticated Oxonian. I was at my office for the most part. One day, I came home to find Julian, boiling and ladling his snotty handkerchiefs in a big soup pot.

"Julian, what in the hell are you doing with my soup pot? It's disgusting". He looked at me in chipper spirit, "We always do this is England."

"If the upper classes soil their food pots with snot rags, what do the lower classes do?"

"They don't use handkerchiefs."

Julian's creditors began to call the house phone. Dear Edith, from the travel agency, wanted her payment for Julian's air tickets. Woodward & Lothrop called for payment on underwear and apparel purchases. Chevy Chase Liquors wanted a hefty sum for Julian's wine provisions. Julian had managed to charm all of these shops to extend credit, much like Rawdon Crawley in *Vanity Fair*.

My response to these numerous calls would be, I have no idea where Mr. Knox is at the moment."

At first I would cover for him, as he declined to take these calls. When they became a nuisance to me, Julian vanished to his hide-outs in Georgetown, often with his less taxing creditors.

At first, it was difficult to admonish him to pay his debts. I did not want to turn off the tap of his cheerful company. Later, when it became imperative to counsel him, it was useless because for Julian, fortune was always around the corner. Finally, as creditor calls exploded it became impossible to speak to him because he vanished.

Stories came my way about Julian's troubled straits. He had to sell his beautiful Rover. Finally, I heard that he went back to England. This was confirmed months later when I heard his cheerful transatlantic voice, "Milton, dear fellow, so sorry that I had to leave in a rush, but I head to clinch an impressive job offer in London. All is well, and I am back home with Jillian. Could you kindly pack a few of my things that I left in your house? I will send you the address here. So many thanks for your kindness and my best to all."

I was delighted to receive a gift package from Julian. It was a costly antique John Dodd violin bow, sent according to his style without provenance or proof of purchase. Shortly afterwards the sad news arrived in a call from his wife Jillian. Julian died of a bleeding stomach hemorrhage. Greta and I were in deep remorse at his passing. We never believed that we would not see him again. Like a winged elf, he migrated to Faerun.

Conviviality: Bill Hawks

"The joy of being with kinsmen in a foreign land" Anonymous

Bill was an early and close American friend in Beijing during the first decade of my business in China, until his untimely death in 2008. He served as deputy to Ambassador James Sasser, until the Sasser's departure in 1999 after the election of George W. Bush. While Sasser intended to return home, his final days were difficult following the accidental U.S. bombing of the Chinese Embassy in Belgrade, during the U.S. military action in Serbia. Following this unfortunate incident, the Chinese Government organized demonstrations at the U.S. Embassy in Beijing.

When Ambassador Sasser returned to the U.S., Bill remained in Beijing as president of the American Chamber of Commerce and as a consultant to American businesses in China. He was introduced to me by our mutual friend Laura Utley, a brilliant and charming philanthropist who was in Beijing frequently at the time. Laura headed her own private environment foundation and gave generously to China's environmental improvement. Bill was a tall, handsome and robust Tennessean. He had a generous and outgoing personality, filled with good humor, intelligence, and tact.

Laura and I had met in Washington, D.C., at a private luncheon at the home of Chinese Ambassador Li Xiaoxing. It was a foursome – the ambassador, his wife, Laura and me. The ambassador appreciated Laura's dedication to China and the China concerts that I produced with the Washington Symphony Orchestra during his tenure in Washington. Laura and I were delighted to meet each other and agreed to an early meeting in Beijing. She was eager to introduce me to her friend Bill Hawks.

Laura traveled frequently to Beijing, and she, Bill, and I regularly got together for dinner at the St. Regis Hotel, and at parties and events. We shared a love of music, business, people, and politics, and the special joy and humor of three American foreigner friends of

China, learning and loving its ways. It was a blessing to have such delightful and instructive American pals in Beijing.

As Bill and I became more confident in our friendship, I told Bill about my plan to establish a Sino-U.S Business Council (SUBC) in Washington. He thought it was a great idea, so I solicited his partnership in the effort. Mainland Chinese business leaders visiting the United States are insulated from the outside world by a triple shield of government oversight, language barriers, and the ubiquitous presence of overseas Chinese "cousins," who blocked their direct contact with American executives for the financial benefit of their own mediation.

The Council would have a research arm and conduct seminars on different industry trends and investment opportunities. It would not be a lobbying group, but would operate as an educational and social society, like other international business councils that Japan, Germany, France and other countries operate in Washington.

The commercial counselor of the Chinese embassy in Washington was overwhelmed by requests for trade and investment assistance, both from the American and Chinese side. He was a good friend with a long tenure in Washington who supported my idea as a positive complement to his own efforts. He was also Bill's friend. The Council would have to be independent of the Chinese government and financially supported by Chinese business leaders.

With the Chinese embassy's support in hand, I introduced the plan in a speech in Beijing before some of China's top business leaders. They responded with enthusiasm. By and large, Chinese business leaders were eager for direct personal and social relations with American business. Opportunities were now of a scale that exceeded their "cousins'" intervention, which too often was a shell game of family consultants who had no real contact with potential American partners. Mainland business people needed an independent and professional social space that could nurture direct social and personal relationships with American business leaders and make them comfortable with corporate and entrepreneurial strangers. Simply put, they needed new business friends in America.

The leaders at my meeting in Beijing wanted to subscribe to the Council if I could set it up as a private body with central government approval. Bill and I spent a good deal of time in meetings and preparing documents. We touched all bases in Beijing and Washington.

I did not want the Council to be an extension of my company, but rather a well-staffed Non Government Organization (NG). Nor did I want to play any operational role. We viewed the effort as a sole benefit to Sino-American business relations. Bill would run the Beijing office, and we would find a distinguished Chinese-American with a corporate background to run the Washington office.

Our plan was set back by the tragedy of Bill's affliction with cancer. He returned to the U.S. for chemotherapy and seemed, after four months, to have beaten his foe into remission. He came back to Beijing more eager than ever to forge ahead with the Council. Laura, Bill, and I resumed our joyful conviviality. Sadly he died within three months of his return, and with his death the Council plan lost his respected leadership in Beijing.

To this day, Chinese business friends ask me about the Council and urge me to get it going. I have not found an able surrogate for Bill to manage the Council in Beijing. The Council is on hold, waiting for a new partner.

Bill had a very happy life in Beijing. He was a diplomat who became a businessman and took to China like a duck to water. He made his livelihood as a consultant, but always kept his eye on the political aim of building good will and mutual advantage between the U.S. and China. He succeeded in his business because he was known and respected by the Chinese as a man who had China's interests at heart. He was respected by the American establishment because it felt he had America's interest at heart. Bill was a master diplomat who favored the underdog. At that time, China was the underdog.

Laura and I continue our friendship in New York. We reminisce about our happy times in the old Beijing days when personal generosity and goodwill could make a difference. Today, China is too rich for personal foreign generosity. The U.S. is too fearful of China to tolerate American personal intimacy with China.

China: Cao "Tiger" Hu

Cao "Tiger" Hu is President of Kotler Marketing China. Tiger has been with me since 1999, when I first came to China for EMKT, a Chinese training company, hoping to be the first provider of marketing services to Chinese companies after the opening of China's market economy in 1982. This young English-speaking and Canadian-educated MBA in marketing was assigned as my interpreter and travel guide in my early travels throughout China for speeches and business meetings.

Tiger came from a scientific family and earned a Master of Science in in biochemistry from the University of Wuhan, prior to receiving his MBA in Ottawa. He then returned to China to work for Henkel, a major German specialty chemical company headquartered in Tianjin. There, he cut his teeth marketing Henkel detergents to the China domestic market.

Tiger's father was a Chinese PhD who came to Purdue University in 1986 for post-doctoral work on DNA. He took his wife and his older son to Layfette, Indiana, leaving Tiger and his sister in China with watchful grandparents. Each year, in that time frame of the

1980s approximately 60,000 young Chinese, primarily science and engineering students, studied in the United States.

Following the 1989 Tiananmen Square protests, many Chinese undergraduate and graduate students left China to seek refuge in the United States, many of whom were granted permanent residence. Unlike them, Tiger's father returned to China to reunite with his family. He had his ups and downs in the political turmoil of post Tiananmen China, but eventually started a medical diagnostic business in Zhengzhou, the capital city of Henan province in central China.

In 1999, Tiger moved from Henkel to EMKT to sell its marketing training programs. He was 24 at the time, and is still a young man today at 43. One of his reasons for moving to EMKT was the opportunity to work with me and learn the Kotler approach to strategic marketing.

Tiger is a brilliant young man with an engaging personality, boundless energy, and constant good humor. Chinese business leaders like to deal with him because of his smarts and optimism. He manages many projects along with our 50 staff members in Beijing and Shenzhen. Beyond management and business development, he trains our young MBA associates in the practice of strategic marketing. They have read the textbooks, but have little business experience. Everything that I know about marketing I learned from my older brother, Philip Kotler, the S.C. Johnson Distinguished Professor of International Marketing at the Kellogg School of Management at Northwestern University. Philip's vast marketing knowledge, combined with my 20 years in American business, enabled me to educate Tiger about the fine points of strategic marketing. Tiger is an exceptionally quick study. He reads the literature, listens to my advice, and grasps practical insights to effectively run our business. As a result, he has successfully passed along his practical experience and marketing know-how to our capable Chinese staff.

Tiger's wife, Tracy, who was also educated in Canada, is a successful private banker, and proud mother of their daughter, Dora. Family is paramount in China. Fortunately, the parental void caused by Tracy's banking duties and Tiger's frequent travel, taking him throughout China and to other international destinations for business development and investment, is filled by their parents. Like many modern Chinese couples, who are both working; retired parents take care of their grandchildren. Tiger, Tracy, and their daughter Dora fully utilize China's two annual vacation periods to share their time together as a family.

Like most educated Chinese, Tiger is well-mannered and appears cheerful, despite chronic physical pain from an autoimmune disorder. He manages to mask the anxiety and frustration that every Chinese business person faces. An explosion of temper, which is common in U.S. business, is rare in China. When Chinese people explode, they usually do this en masse, as in the case of the vandalizing protests in 1999 against the U.S. Embassy in Beijing, following the accidental U.S. bombing of the Chinese Embassy in Belgrade, Serbia, during the Kosovo War. Such rancor took place on a far larger scale in the period 1966 to 1976, during the Red Guards assaults during the Cultural Revolution.

Tiger's great personal qualities have garnered him numerous close friends that he can count on for the pleasure of good company and the ways and means of building business fortunes together. Many are old friends from home-town schools and universities. A Chinese person may have 10 such friends who will give them the shirt off their back. In turn, each of them has the same number of friends, who become collateral friends of their friend's friend. This is a very powerful network for business, social, and personal life in a land of decades of a one-child policy and high mobility. Friends pool their resources and form new business partnerships very quickly. We have no such social fabric in the U.S., where our risk capital for start-up enterprise generally comes from the extended family circle or collateralized finance.

The point of this story is that Tiger is the gold standard for a general manager and partner for an American business in China. I never could have found him if I had to look for him. He found me. The best way to find a "Tiger" is to establish a brand presence in China with a unique business value for China. People will hear about you and talk to their friends about your venture. By word of mouth, you may be lucky enough to find a "Tiger." There is no way for an American to run a business in China without a Chinese compatriot.

The Kotler name was prominent in China industry because of the acclaimed marketing work of my brother, Philip. His leading text, Marketing Management, was translated into Mandarin in Singapore in the 1970s, bringing him to the attention of Chinese business executives. His book was a must read for business executives when China became a market economy, with Chinese characteristics, in 1982. The unique Kotler brand positioned me to work exclusively for Chinese companies, enabling them to compete with the West.

Tiger and I have constantly adapted our business model in China to fast-changing market conditions. For the first decade of our enterprise, KMG provided strategic marketing and branding consultation to Chinese State-owned and private companies. Our clients included China Aviation Industries (AVIC), Merchant Group, Ping An Insurance, Tencent, China Resources Company, and other top State-owned and private companies.

For the past decade, our business has added the planning, design, financing, and operation of high tech parks. We currently operate Kotler Medical Park in Dongguan for medical devices, and are developing Kotler Radical Innovation Park in Zhengzhou for advanced manufacturing technology. We attract foreign enterprises to our facilities that wish to locate in the Chinese market.

Tiger and I have shared many adventures in this land of abundant opportunity. We have weathered storms and sailed in calm seas and built a wide circle of Chinese associates, partners, investors, staff, clients, and government officials. We have also brought a large number of American and European consultants, companies, and institutions to China to assist us in our commercial endeavors.

I have spent 10 years learning enough of the Chinese language, Mandarin, to get by. Tiger is completely fluent in English. For the first 10 years, Tiger spared no effort to keep up with me. For the past decade, I have spared no effort to keep up with him and out excellent staff. Many of our past staff have gone on to start their own companies. Several own or lead listed companies on Chinese and American trading exchanges. In managing our company, Tiger has encouraged our staff to become entrepreneurial and spread their own wings. His vision has been to build the wealth and prosperity of China, not to accrete personal fortune. He lives with a deep sense of responsibility to his family, his company, to others, to his country, and in his quest for personal wisdom. He personifies the new

Chinese person of science, enterprise, and ambitious spirit that young men and women in America must compete and cooperate with if they desire to succeed in their sphere. He is my greatest hope for a happy future of good relations between China and the United States.

The purpose of this story is to convey to my American readers the high caliber and humanity of young Chinese entrepreneurs. We have a mistaken and fanciful view of the Chinese people that is born of our ignorance and prejudice. We had better correct this misunderstanding before it redounds to our economic and perhaps political detriment.

Common Sense: Maurice Kotler

"Common sense is genius dressed in its working clothes" Ralph Waldo Emerson

My father, Maurice Kotler, was a man of good sense and sound judgment in practical matters. He was mindful of the consequences of action and was concerned that his sons should act in a manner that would lead to their honor, prosperity and happiness. He was a man of common sense.

There are certain predicates of common sense, principally that there is a common world. One can only have sound judgment in practical matters if there is a common world that looks at and weighs action and consequence in a like manner. If a human community has norms, then common sense works. If the community is fractured and diverse, common sense is only elusive and dubious.

My father's world was a Russian Jewish community in Chicago. All of his friends were merchants, who shared a Jewish culture of English, Yiddish and Russian. This was a sufficient generational community for common sense. Their children and in some case their wives aspired to be Yankees.

This brings us to the other fundamentals about common sense. Common sense is always under siege by a new generation. Every generation aims to unseat its parent's world. What was common sense to my father and his peers was not necessarily common sense to his children. Common sense can only continue for matters that transcend generation and perdure. It is more relevant to elemental human goals like survival, prosperity, and respect, than for effervescent matters of pleasure, fashion, and taste.

My father was born in Nezhin, Russia, in 1905 and died in Chicago in 1981. He was born into a merchant class and died in a merchant class. His languages spanned Yiddish, Hebrew, Russian, and English. His religious beliefs spanned Orthodox Judaism and Conservative Judaism. His political beliefs spanned capitalism, socialism, Zionism, and the Democratic Party.

When I was 10, my father took me to visit my Uncle Dave on Division Street. "Let's visit Uncle Dave!" It was a Saturday noon in springtime. We walked three blocks from our apartment on Evergreen Avenue to the main commercial street of the neighborhood. We came to the pool hall nestled between delicatessens, shoe stores, butchers, produce shops, and hat and apparel stores.

My father took me into pool hall and headed for a concealed door. He opened the door and we walked in to a maelstrom of yelling, drinking and gambling. There were a hundred men at card tables gaming away in a fever of delirium. To me, the noise was deafening, the smell of liquor noxious, and the physical agitation frightening. We saw Dave and approached him. He bid my father a desultory greeting and brushed my head with a perfunctory smile. We were disturbing him.

Uncle Dave was my funny uncle and my father's business partner in the St. Louis Fish Market. Like my father, he had three sons, and unlike my father, a bedraggled wife. My mother was beautiful. My father was devastated by his younger brother's gambling addiction. Dave neglected his wife and children, and was truant from the business. There was a strong love between the brothers and a shared devotion to their mother, my grandmother, Gretal. I grew up knowing that there was something wrong with Uncle Dave. Now I saw it and my father brought me to see it.

Uncle Dave and his fellow card players were in a feverish frenzy. They yelled, imbibed, and laughed hysterically at each other and at others. They all smoked into a tobacco penumbra that enveloped their table. It was fury, fury, fury to a 10 year old! So this was gambling! My father wished his brother well, greeted his cronies, and introduced me as Dave's nephew. They obliged Dave with a cursory compliment to me, "Good looking kid!" I was wincing at the stink of the place when father bid farewell. We left the gambling den for the commercial air of the street, a redolent mixture of fresh air and the aroma of corned beef coming from the delicatessens.

We walked home in silence. Dad never uttered a word about the ruin of gambling. No exhortation, no preaching. Action spoke louder than words. He respected my little mind and I grew up repulsed by gambling. How's that for common sense?

In my teen years, Dad bought an Oldsmobile vehicle that had many mechanical problems. He called the dealer and appealed for a replacement car. The dealer, a local, was unresponsive. Dad finally decided that he had to take matters into his own hands. He bought a large poster board and wrote these words: "Rothman Oldsmobile sold me a lemon. Beware!"

On a Saturday, which is the biggest sales day for auto dealers: and a day when his own store was closed, he picketed the dealership in a business suit, marching to and fro in front of the Rothman dealership for the entire afternoon. He was like a union picketer in the days when people respected the unions. As a well-known neighborhood merchant, friends stopped to chat with Dad and listened to his story. No one wanted a lemon! People who were about to enter the auto dealership turned away.

Dad did this for two Saturdays, until Rothman called. He was urged to stop and in return would be given a replacement vehicle with an additional guarantee. The matter was finished. Dad prevailed with good common sense and a lot of effort.

My father suffered severe pain for from gallstones. There were no pain relief medicines that that could abate his pain. The doctor recommended surgery, but my father was reluctant, He had to be at his store. He knew that surgery was necessary, but he tried to stall the procedure for the sake of his business. He devised his own remedy.

When the sharp pain came, he would knock his head against the wall, so that his milder head pain would offset the greater gallstone pain. I remember myself as a youngster startled at my father's flagellation. He explained the procedure. I was astounded by his courage.

My father was 12 when the Czar Nicholas, II abdicated in 1917, following the Russian Revolution. In the early spring of 1918, when my father was 13, his uncle in Nezhin, Ukraine, a commercial city near Kiev, gave him and his younger brother David two large suitcases filled with fiat rubles and placed them on the Trans-Siberian train to Vladivostok. "Do not get off the train until the end of the line. Trade the rubles for gold and come back."

Maurice and David followed orders. They reached far-eastern Russia before the Czar and his family were executed on June, 1918. The ruble still had value in the Czarist East. They made the trade and returned with the gold to Nezhin. That one transaction saved his mother and siblings from desolation in the following years of World War 1 (WWI), the Revolution and Civil War violence.

Dad's father had migrated to America in 1913 to prepare the way for bringing his family to the new world. WWI trumped that plan. His wife, Gretal, and the four children were stuck in the Ukraine to endure the bloody war and ensuing revolution. Gretal remained to manage the family business until their forestalled emigration to the U.S., but during this period, there was no trade. The family lived on the gold until 1921, when my grandfather sent an agent to wrest his family from the havoc and bring them to Chicago.

This was a case of ethnic common sense. What was imminent to some Russian Jews of the Ukraine was unimaginable to Czarist Russians of the Far East. Grandma Gretal's brother saw a new age coming. Like an alchemist he enlisted two nephews to turn paper into gold.

In 1946, auto production was resumed in America. My dad bought a new green Plymouth to replace our 1936 Dodge and in 1948 we were off to California to see the sights and visit our relatives who had moved to the west coast.

It was no easy matter to get from Chicago to Los Angeles before the days of the Interstate Highway System. You had to get a stack of travel directions from the American Automobile Association (AAA), and navigate to your destination through twists and turns of city streets, country roads, state roads, and misleading signs. We lodged at makeshift motels through the Great Plains states, up through the Rockies on roads with no guard rails, and down to the coast until we arrived in the land of milk and honey.

Palm trees, palm trees. What a breathless sight for a 12 year old boy from Chicago. Where were the coal dust and brick apartments of Chicago? Not here in a land of white stucco homes and exotic trees and plants. Where was the gloom and chill of Chicago winters in this land of sunshine and warmth? This was heaven to me and my family.

Dad fell in love with the place. I had never seen him so happy and invigorated. We visited the Hollywood Studios and ocean beaches of Santa Monica. We visited my cousins who seemed to me like a different breed, gleeful, not bookish. Their parents prospered in sunshine. How paradoxical! To Chicagoans, success required sacrifice to freezing rain and forbidding snow. Could this land be real?

Our motel was modern, unlike the dingy digs along the way. There was a swimming pool. There were no swimming pools in Chicago, except in high schools and fancy hotels. This was ubiquitous luxury and luxury bit my dad.

We gathered one day and Dad declared that our motel was for sale. He wanted to buy it. My brothers and I were thrilled at the idea of our exodus from Chicago to this blessed place. Mother was reluctant. "What about our family and friends, your mother and brother? What about your business?" My dad was heedless, so enlivened by sunny Los Angeles. Mother obliged and said, okay. Dad spoke to the motel owner. There were about 15 units, enough to make a starting living and expand from there. The price was $25,000. Dad wrote a check and held it for a night of thought.

The next morning we heard his decision. "No, we return to Chicago." The change was too abrupt. Leaving his mother, siblings, friends, and business was too unsettling. "We will visit California again. Our home is in Chicago."

Back in Chicago, my brothers and I went on to the University of Chicago and successful professional careers. My father's business flourished to a comfortable new home in Skokie and later retirement in Miami. Mother returned to her sister and brother; dad to his pinochle friends and beloved synagogue. The path in Chicago was clear The path in Los Angeles enticing but uncertain. He had common sense to heed to mother's caution.

Dad brought home troubling stories about his partner, Boris Mellen. As if his problems with his gambling brother and partner Dave were not enough to distress him, he also had problems with his partner Boris. Boris took cash from the register when my father wasn't looking.

"What are you going to do?" said mother. "Nothing," answered Dad. This went on for years. Every recounted episode, invited the same "What are you going to do?" comment from mother. Dad's response was always the same, "Nothing!"

When I was in high school, I felt entitled to probe deeper. "Dad, you can't always say 'nothing' when you keep railing against Boris for his thievery. "My son," he responded, "Boris is important to the business. He gets the best quality and prices from our wholesalers. I am great with our customers. He is great with our suppliers. We couldn't operate without him; just like he could not hold on to our customers without me."

I had enough Talmudic training to ask, "Please, tell me why you are saying that you will do nothing about a thief." He looked deeply at me. "So long as there is enough money in the cash register for our family, I will keep the business sailing ahead." More common sense!

Here is an episode of my father's guidance that was common sense at the time, and seems ridiculous today. Common sense changes as the common world changes. My father was a professional soccer player on the Maccabees team in Chicago before he went into business. He began playing as a kid in Russia, and continued as an athlete when he came to Chicago. He came from a merchant family that was half devout and half secular, and spiked with the bug of socialism that promised liberty for Jews within the bosom of Zionism and Russian brotherhood. Pushkin freed his mind and soccer freed his body for sport, instead of incessant genuflecting prayer.

When Dad married mother, he gave up soccer, which paid very little, and went into commerce. He had to make a living and support a family. At mother's urging Dad set aside his uniform and cleats and carried his scares into a life of business. He had a tough go at it, like all the young Jewish guys on the block, who had a Jewish wife and children, and who had to make a living. He succeeded and prospered. He loved soccer and athleticism, but had to face the facts of common sense. At $25 a game there was no future for him in soccer. He continued his love of the game and took me and Phil to games every weekend. We liked the heroics that we saw, but Dad warned us. "You must never waste your time on sports. You future is law, medicine, or science. Don't waste your time in sports."

So Philip, Neil, and I grew up as mental workers and succeeded with a career and family life of which my father and mother were proud. Of course, at the age of 84 my body is a wreck, but my mind is as agile as a gazelle. I miss common sense. It was precious and effective in the common world that has passed, and has no place in this present world of fractured diversity and contrived community, where the tiny worlds of invented identity flit for a moment and die like fireflies.

Hospitality: South Haven, Michigan

The day after the school year ended our family departed for South Haven, Michigan. Father packed us and everything we would need that summer into the car. Off we went for a three hour drive southeast from Chicago to our resort destination. We would remain there until the weekend before school resumed. Many families with young children spent summers in the countryside, and not just the rich. There were few affordable summer camps for kids in those days. Few women worked – they stayed at home to care for their children. In the summertime, fathers would work during the week and join his wife and children at the resorts on the weekends. Aside from a respite from the summer's higher temperatures in the city, a compelling reason for this exodus was the plague of polio, measles, whooping cough, and chicken pox that racked dense cities before the introduction of antibiotics and vaccines.

South Haven in the 1940s was a Jewish resort town for rich,

middle class and working class Chicagoans. Today it is a posh resort town for everyone rich enough to vacation there. In the old days, the place was cheap and hygienic. Dad deposited us at Kessie's Resort, a resort in name only. This Jewish summer respite had resorts that ranged from luxury to bare bones. Kessie's was at the lower end of the spectrum. It was a big old rooming house with eight sleeping rooms on the second floor and another eight rooms on the third floor. The kitchen, dining room, and common room, as well as owner's quarters, were on the first floor.

The sleeping rooms did not have toilets or baths, only tap water sinks. There were two full shared bathrooms on each floor with tubs and toilets. Our room was occupied by four bodies during the week – Mother, Philip, me, and later Neil, with Dad making it five on the weekend These were sleeping rooms, with two double beds, one crib for Neil, a dresser drawer, and an armoire. There were no chairs or desks. All living was done in the first floor common room, dining room, screened porch and outdoors. There were farms on both sides of the resort and a dense thicket forest behind Kessie's building.

Our vacation sleeping room was a parody of our small four-room, one bedroom apartment in the city. At the time, there was an acute housing shortage in Chicago. There were no large apartments for working people in Chicago during the Depression and the end of World War II. Though five people in a four room city apartment compared to Kessie's tight sleeping quarters might seem like a step backward, for us it felt like a step forward because of the welcoming outdoors, the beach and the comforting summer breeze. We were free from contagious city diseases and had Lake Michigan for swimming and fishing.

This brings us to the first floor common area and the outdoors. On the first floor there was a large kitchen where each family shared several refrigerators and ice boxes; as well as a dry goods shelf for packaged goods. There were cutting tables, work tables, ovens, kitchen sinks, pots and pans and every necessary utensil for cooking. The large dining room accommodated eight tables for family dining. Each family had their own table or shared a table.

There was a piano and sitting chairs in the large living room, or common area, along with a modest stage riser and dancing area for entertainment. Husbands came every Friday night for the weekend and returned to their shops and businesses every Monday at dawn. My father played the piano after dinner. Other parents and kids would play the accordion, clarinet, or violin and the families would sing and dance. There was a large screened in porch that wrapped around the front and side of the house. On the porch there were tables for card games and sitting and rocking chairs for relaxation and snoozing. The men played cards, Pinochle and Poker far into the weekend nights with thousands of moths circling the electric bulbs. There also was fly stick paper rolls hanging everywhere to catch the ever-present bugs. The women played Mahjong and new card games like Canasta and Kalooki.

People talked on the porch with hand fans, amidst the whizzing noise of electric fans, while they laughed and gossiped. Outside there were lawn chairs and picnic tables for table games, card games, food, and chatter. There also was a lawn area for croquet.

In the back of the resort house was a wooded area filled with Sassafras scrub trees growing in a sandy loam, where the children played in the woods, if they were not swimming in the turquoise water of Lake Michigan at South Beach.

Most of the adults were Russian immigrants who shared a common bond of meaning: they had left a tough life behind them, including the horrors of war, but they had hope for the future with family love at their sides, and perhaps luck just around the corner. As fully assimilated "Yankee" kids, we watched them inquisitively and played our own games.

If our circumstances at Kessie's were tight, Aunt Jenny's abode was jam-packed. Jenny was mother's aunt. She and her husband, Louie, lived permanently in South Haven. They had a small store across from the high school called "Louie's Store — Jenny's Famous Hamburgers." Aunt Jenny, Uncle Louie, their daughters, Phyllis and Esther, and Jenny's Chicago sisters, Ruchel and Yetta and their husbands, as well their closest friend, Minnie and her husband Sam, all lived during the summers in an apartment in the back of the store.

The store itself was tiny. There was a small counter with candy, gum, and cigarettes at the side of the entrance door, and two four person booths for eating hamburgers. In the back of the customer section was the kitchen, where Aunt Jenney mixed her hamburger meats, chopped her onions, made her French fries, and talked continuously to Yetta and Ruchel. The three sisters always stood side by side. In 1921, they had brought Mother, then seven, to America from Berdichev, Russia, and raised her.

A door divided the store from the back apartment, where somehow everyone lived. Years later, Ruchel and her husband Ellie built a tiny one room house in the backyard, where they slept. Before this was built, somehow, everyone slept in the apartment behind the store. Above the store, there was an apartment rented to the Rabbi of the South Haven Synagogue.

In great aunt Jenny's living quarters there was a dining room which also served as a sewing room with a mannequin for her dress making. Aunts Ruchel and Yetta were dressmakers, who were always cutting fabric and sewing. There was barely room to move between the three sisters, the mannequin, rolls of fabric, and the pins and needles. This paraphernalia was magically removed every evening for a sit down meal.

To the front right of this room was a small living room with a couch and sitting chairs where I did my serious talking with aunt Jenny's children, my cousins, Phyllis and Esther, and my older brother Philip. Esther was the oldest. Philip and Phyllis were the same age. Since Phyliss was genealogically Philip's aunt once removed, they seemed like cousins to me. The girls were very intelligent. Esther was light-hearted and sensitive, and Phyllis was a hard headed intellectual like Philip. Phyllis subscribed to *Foreign Affairs* magazine at a time in my life when I thought that Jews were not allowed to subscribe. Phyllis was eventually Philip's date at his high school prom. They are fast friends to this day.

To the rear right of the dining or sewing room was a bedroom which I assumed belonged to Jenny and Louie. The girls slept on the pull out couch in the living room. There was only one other room, a large screened porch in the rear where Ruchel, Yetta, Minnie and their husbands slept on cots.

In later years, I asked Phyllis how they managed in this congestion. She could not recall how they bed, fed and entertained 10 people in a space of no more than 800 square feet. Our family could afford to stay at Kessie's resort in our 200 square foot bedroom, but

Jenny would have squeezed us in if necessary. We were used to small spaces with our four-room Chicago apartment. Small spaces seem big to small children. Aspiring adults lived with a horizon of larger spaces. The hospitality of family, friends, and a prosperous country got us from where we were to a more ample destiny. Today, there is a flourishing international hospitality industry of grand hotels, sunset coves, radiant beeches, martinis, and an affordable high life. In my 1940s youth, hospitality was makeshift, gracious, and humble.

Adventure: A Jewish Tom Sawyer

Can I tell you about the adventures of a Jewish Tom Sawyer at Von Humboldt Elementary School in the Humboldt Park neighborhood in the 1940s? I think that I should. They revolve around escaping from the usual school work to help teachers live their daily lives, and in the process learn a bit about politics, vandalism, and the horrors of industrial life.

Oysters

At the age of 12, when I was in the seventh grade, a bright and charming student could rise to the call of duty. In this case, it was to help Ms. Clinnin, the principal of Von Humboldt Elementary school. Ms. Clinnin was the primus inter pares of the Lace-Curtain Irish school principals and teachers who ruled Chicago's elementary schools. They were responsible for educating and disciplining thousands of immigrant children from Eastern European countries –

first-generation Jewish and Catholics kids from Russian, Polish, Czech, Hungarian, Greek, Serb, and Ukrainian families. They were a sorority of nuns in secular habits who wore long black dresses, pince-nez glasses, and brooches. They were the Irish girls too good for the Irish fellows, probably too good and not sufficiently narrowed minded to become real nuns. So while their devotional sisters ran the parochial schools in Chicago, these ladies ran the public schools.

Their dresses came in different sizes as they advanced in their career. They started out thin and expanded with age and status. Ms. Clinnin was the largest of the lot. Her deputy, Ms. Waters, was slightly trimmer, but not by much. Ms. Clinnin needed help. Their dresses had to picked up downtown from the Lane Bryant department store on State Street that specialized in the larger sizes. Their cakes had to be picked up Henrici's, a classy place that was then one of the oldest and finest restaurants in Chicago. It was located on Randolph Street in the heart of the Theater District. In those days, I was the courier. As a trustworthy seventh grader, it was my duty to go downtown and pick up Ms. Clinnin's wares – a duty delegated to teachers in cahoots with Ms. Clinnin, who would recommend couriers intelligent enough to do the task, and tacit enough not to report these chores to their parents or neighborhood busybodies who had their nose in politics.

"Who can I trust to get my dresses and cakes?"

The chorus responded: "Mickey Kotler will like the trip. He'll not say a word. You can depend on him." With a taste for adventure beyond my neighborhood, I began my career in political prudence.

With a dollar tip and two nickels for the street car, I ventured downtown for Ms. Clinnin via the street car on Division Street. In the course of my seventh and eighth grades, I must have made these trips to the Loop a dozen times. Each trip meant a day away from the academics of school, which did not seem to bother my teachers. It certainly didn't bother me since I was not learning anything anyway. It was a confirmation of my importance. How many kids with a dollar in their pocket could be relied upon to reach Lane Bryant, enter the store, find the right counter, present the pick-up note, and say with confidence, "I have a note from Ms. Clinnin to pick up her dress?"

My itinerary took me on a walk from school on Hirsh Street to Division Street, where I boarded the streetcar for the 30-minute nickel trolley ride to Lane Bryant, where I went to the dress department to accomplish my secret mission. At the time, I was reading E. Phillip Oppenheimer's WW I spy novels that embraced the espionage of my mission. I would take the package and walk to Henrici's, the second part of my secret mission.

In the store front window of Henrici's, I saw a big burly black man shucking oysters to the delight of passer-by. Transfixed, I stared at the shucker as he smiled at his work, scrapping oysters from their calcium beds. Each oyster was scooped into a half shell and laid on a platter with its five brethren, as waiters moved the platters to customer's tables. Though we never ate this *Traif* (non- Kosher) at home, I was familiar with oysters since my father sold them at his fish store in a gentile neighborhood. Dad would dish out shucked oysters from a gallon canister and pack this stuff for his Swedish customers; but he never shucked an oyster.

We ate shrimp, bacon and spareribs at our home but never oysters. Oysters and crabs were beyond the perimeter of permissible *Traif.* There had be a final barrier between the Jewish and *goyishe* world – a last stop that could not be crossed before falling into the abyss of apostasy and everything that would follow from that – like marrying a s*hikse* (a non-Jewish girl). Hence, the sublime intrigue of the oyster.

I gazed long enough to be emboldened to cross the barrier of my mission. Here I was – an official truant on a mission of trust from Ms. Clinnin's concealed purpose. I was an operative agent in a covert act that violated public duty – sending an 12 year old kid downtown during school hours with specific instructions to pick up personal goods for a public employee without telling a soul about it. It was a delicious excitement that Tom Sawyer would have enjoyed.

The placard in the window read: "75 cents for six oysters." I entered Henrici's, first to pick up Ms. Clinnin's cake order before I took a seat at a table for two. The waiter asked for my order. "Six oysters, please." He returned with a platter of oysters laid circularly on a bed of lettuce with a little fork and red sauce and lemon in the center.

I poked the first oyster with my fork; but it did not hold. Unlike a piece of beef that you could securely plug and lift to your mouth, the oyster fell off the fork. When I finally secured the beastie, I brought it to my mouth. What in the world would it taste like? Is this really the end of my heritage? Too late to turn back, I slid it into my mouth. It has no taste, and I did not know what to do with it. Do you chew this slimy thing or swallow it? Does it dissolve in your mouth or do you shove it down your throat?

While trying to decide, I observed how other patrons ate their oysters. I followed suit, but the slimy thing slithered in my throat. I gagged, grabbed my throat, and bent my chest. The thing popped out of my mouth. How do I get it back in so that it would stay in? The waiter rushed to the table. "Are you alright?" "I'm fine," I wheezed. I don't feel well today. "

"You better not eat any more."

"I guess not," I said, gaping at the oyster platter with remorse, I paid my 75 cents and left. Twenty years would pass before I had my next oyster. It was delicious, and I married a gentile gal.

Gun Smoke

Following my downtown missions for Ms. Clinnin, my second major assignment was a surveillance job for Ms. Parker, a very pretty lady who was my seventh grade teacher. Someone had slashed her the tires of her car that was parked across the street from our school. She needed help. Someone had to stake out her car and identify the vandalizing culprits.

Naturally, she selected me, given my extra mural experiences on behalf of Ms. Clinnin. This job needed more than a trusted courier. It needed a defense team. I asked Ms. Parker if Tony, my friend and classmate, could assist me. Tony, a talented cartoonist, was a tall Ukrainian kid. Soon, we were both dispatched.

Ms. Parker's car was a green Chevy that was parked on Hirsh Street between Mrs. Laikin's grocery store and Wojciechowski's Funeral Home. She took us to her car at 10 a.m. and sat us in the front seats. "Keep your heads low, so they don't see you before you see them." We ducked beneath the steering wheel and the glove compartment.

What plan did she have for sealing us in this supine position until 3 p.m.? "You can listen to the radio, but keep it soft." After, she showed us how to activate the radio without running the engine, she gave us a bag of candy bars. Tony and I were set for the day – five hours of watchfulness.

We played and pretended. I can't remember how we whiled away the time. At lunch time, kids passed us as we kept undercover. Ms. Parker showed up with lunch sandwiches and milk. "Did anything happen?" "No. Ms. Parker."

We continued to sit under the steering wheel, occasionally rising like a periscope to investigate the terrain. Then, at 2 p.m. it happened. Thump, thump – someone was hitting the car. My heart beat with fear. They're here – whoever they are.

The most important thing was to lock the doors from the inside so they couldn't get in and get us. Our hands elevated to depress the door safety locks. Whoever they were, they could see serpentine arms reaching for the safety locks. Thump, thump! "Who's in there?"

Down we crept, involuting our little bodies into curled balls of flesh on the car floor so they couldn't see us. Though my heart was beating in fear, curiosity got the best of me. I stuck up my head to face the monsters before us. Tony followed. We beheld three honest to goodness *shkotzim* (gentile rascals) beating the car with sticks then rocking the car. "Hey you, get out!"

"Who? Us? Not on your life."

"Come out you god dam shits."

"Not on your life."

Our fear cost Ms. Parker a new set of tires. Pssst – punctures of all four tires! I saw their nasty faces as they shook the car and ran off.

Once they had left, trembling, we somehow steeled ourselves to open the latch and flee the car. We returned to the school and ran into the classroom to report the crime to Ms. Parker. "It happened. They got the tires."

"Oh no," she exclaimed as she ran out with us to the scene of the crime.

"Did you see their faces?"

"Sure enough", I said. What kind of special agent would miss this evidence? This admission did me and Tony in. The next day, Tony and I were ordered to inspect all of the seventh and eighth grade classes, as well as the high school classes in the school district. For the next two days we went to six schools. In each school, the boys were lined up by their teachers. We were flanked by the assistant principal of Von Humboldt and a Chicago police officer.

"Stand up," the teachers commanded. All of the boys stood and moved forward. "These people want to take a good look at you," piped the lady teachers, who relished every opportunity to denigrate their male students as the bums that down deep they thought they were, or would become.

No sighting was made until the last school, where, low and behold, Tony and I spotted the three hooligans who would kill us if we fingered them. I looked at Tony and Tony looked at me. Our eyes glazed at their menacing faces like a feather in the wind – no pauses – no accusations on our part.

"I don't see them"

"You sure?"

"We're sure."

The case of the un-apprehended vandals rested and our silence was set in stone.

The next day, the three thugs showed up in our school yard at recess. "We'll kill you if you squeal." This terror was icing on the cake of prudence. Gratuitous! We would not have squealed.

"No," we assured them. "We'll not squeal."

Slaughter House Blues

Before the days of Eco-Tourism, there was an era of social realism. Enter that period in Chicago, the Hog Butcher of the world! Today, children are likely to take school trips to local bird sanctuaries, recycling plants, Disney Land, or the rain forests of Costa Rica. In the 1940s, Chicago children visited the engines of Chicago's economy – the Commodity Exchange trading pits and the pit of all pits, the bloody pools of the Chicago Stockyards.

Hog Butcher for the World,

Tool Maker, Stacker of Wheat,

Player with Railroads and the Nation's Freight Handler;

Stormy, husky, brawling,

City of the Big Shoulders

Chicago by Carl Sandburg

Our teachers extolled Carl Sandburg. We memorized his bombastic lines. This was preparation for our major seventh grade outing – the trip to Chicago's South Side Stock Yards. School trips were rare in those days. They required buses that were leased from the Chicago transit authority when gas was scarce. Yellow school buses were not common in those days. The trip also required parental volunteers in days before soccer moms, when mothers rarely stuck their noses into school matters. When they did, it was usually to reprimand their wayward child in front of school officials. The closest thing to a PTA meeting was annual visit of parents to identify their child to the teacher. This was not teacher hospitality, the parent's association with their child was more like a police lineup

It was difficult for the Lace Curtin Irish teachers to get cowed immigrant women to help them manage us rascals for a day trip. I remember only four trips – Orchestra Hall in the upper balcony, the Planetarium, the Stock Yards, and the Commodity Exchange.

The Stock Yards were vast and noisy; and above all, malodorous. A stench rose from the charnel house buildings, where cattle, pigs, and sheep were driven from railroad box cars to open pens that crisscrossed the yards – holding pens prior to the slaughter. I still remember the horrendous sound of hysterical mooing, yelps and howls of the animals as they moved to the slaughter house.

The bus took us to a plant in a building where we were led by our teacher and a Hormel Company man up a stairway and onto an observation platform. Cattle were driven up a scaffold in front of our eyes by burly herders, who prodded them forward for a massive knockout blow. The animals were shitting and howling. Once they were bludgeoned, shackles were attached to their feet and they were hoisted onto a moving belt to the next rank of executioners who slit their throats with broad knives. The blood gushed forth into channels. We were delirious. This horror was very exciting to 12 year old kids. This was what life was really about. This was the food on our tables. This made Chicago great.

After this spectacle, we were led back down the steps, so the kids from the next school could see the show. "Wow! Wait until you see what we saw," we acclaimed to the passing kids with our ravenous eyes.

Driving back to school was a nonstop pulsation of hysterical chatter. We talked about what we had seen to each other, to the teacher, and to our parents. Eventually, by evening we assimilated the horror. For the next few days in school, we affirmed our civic pride in Chicago and our poetic praise for Carl Sandberg. The experience branded me with a realism that has ever since tempered my idealistic impulses.

Serenity: Lee Haupt

"I will be calm. I will be mistress of myself." <u>Jane Austen</u>, <u>Sense and Sensibility</u>

Lee Haupt was my dearest friend in Chicago until her death in 2013. We went to the University of Chicago together. She was in English literature and I was in political science. We both taught at Wright Junior College while we were working on our doctoral degrees. Lee loved tennis, horses, and friends. We were very fond of each other. Our relationship veered toward romance, but never quite made it there. Possibly because we were too respectful of each other! She was born in Vienna and carried the gilded art nouveau zeitgeist of Gustav Klimpt in her personal bearing. I carried a free and refreshing new world of Humboldt Park in Chicago in my bearing. She felt cloistered and wanted to be fee. She adored my comfort with freedom. I adored her steadfast taste.

Lee was short and attractive with a taught and wiry figure honed by daily tennis. She had a fertile mind and decisive voice. She brooked no nonsense when it came to matters of the mind and would not tolerate intellectual pretense. She was intensely polite and never compromised her bearing when among fools. Her Viennese taste was cultivated by her family after they escaped Vienna in 1938 and were deposited in the pedestrian life of Chicago's north side.

Lee's father was a physician, her mother a matron, and her sister an artist. Her mother walked Freud's dog in the neighborhood of Berggasse 19 in Vienna's 9th district. Lee could never shake the psychiatric phantoms of that heritage. Her sister was a hysteric, who abandoned her husband and three children to suicide; and Lee always feared that she was next. The psyche of Vienna always haunted Lee.

We had great times together in Hyde Park. Lee had a small circle of sexually dystopian friends with whom we rode horses in Jackson Park and swam in Lake Michigan at the Point promontory. We frolicked on the landscape of the University of Chicago campus and played tennis on the quadrangle courts. The late 1950s was a refreshing time of youthful freedom enwreathed with literary talk. Even in those happy times Lee carried a nervous caution, always on edge that dark forces stalked her. Her escape from Nazi Vienna and the utter destruction of her family's prosperous and genteel existence was a ghost that stalked her daily life. Always watchful, she did her best to sheath this ghost. Her father and mother never adjusted to American life. She did her best to mask the family's longing for their finer life.

Lee needed an anchor in the New World. She thought she found it in the tall, handsome and successful figure of Ralph Stavins. Ralph was a Chicago north side boy, whose father owned a liquor store. Ralph was bound for money and success. He did not have an ounce of finesse, just raw ambition and a needling sense of higher ideals. He was a thriving attorney who could be an avenue for Lee's freedom, as well as a linchpin of safety for Lee and her confounded family — two contradictory desires. They married.

Ralph was very smart, but not educated in any classical sense. He excelled at his legal craft, but could not be enthralled by Mahler, enchanted by Egon Schiele and Gustav Klimt, forewarned by Musil, and suffer like Rilke. Lee had her mission to transform coarse Ralph into a *Richtige mensch*. Ralph whose brilliance was flattered, abandoned law and entered the University of Chicago's political science department, where we met and became friends.

Their marriage lasted three years, until Lee gave up her trial of metamorphosis. Ralph's rawness was cratered in his being. Ralph saw Lee as a maternal mate. He wanted a child and she wanted a count. They divorced, and Lee came to visit me in Washington for a summer of companionship. Eventually, Ralph happily married Chong, a beautiful, intelligent and practical Korean American woman, who respected his material prowess and his mind. They read Trollope together. Chong, polished Ralph in a manner unknown to Lee.

Sam and Janet Rosenkrantz were living in Washington as well. Our old Hyde Park merriment was reset in a new place which Lee thought was a new Vienna in the American Empire. She loved Washington and its political courtiers. It renewed her faith that taste can triumph.

Wistfully, Lee returned to Chicago and to her college teaching. She had a tenured position at the new Chicago City College. God blessed her desultory circumstance with an architectural faculty colleague, Michael Rosen. Michael was a gentleman. He dressed impeccably with J. Press suits, thin bow ties, and a collection of fedoras. Michael was liberally educated and devoted to Bauhaus architecture and furnishings. He had Viennese taste and was a successful architect. They dated and married and lived in a stylish Bauhaus home in Hyde Park. Michael had two children from a prior marriage, to whom Lee fastened her soul with deep affection. She delighted in their children and became, as years passed, a reprised Viennese matron in Hyde Park, Chicago, until she died in 2013.

To this day, Michael pines for his lost love. He has cataloged her writings and published some of her Vienna stories. Like Orpheus, he visits his beloved *Eurydice every gloaming night to bring her back to their home and their eternal love affair.*

෯ ෯ ෯

About the Author

Milton Kotler, at 83, has led a life of varied endeavors. Born in Chicago, Milton spent 12 years (1951-1963) at the University of Chicago in the college, political science department, and the law school. He came to Washington, D.C., as a founding fellow of the Institute for Policy Studies (1963-1976), where he principally devoted his thought and action to urban affairs, civil rights, neighborhood organizing, community development, and neighborhood government.

He organized and led the National Association of Neighborhoods (1975-1981), which played an important political and legislative role in democratic models of local government. He was a principal legislative advisor on the origination and implementation of Washington, D.C.'s Advisory Neighborhood Commissions.

Mr. Kotler left the world of public policy in 1981 to enter the world of business as a strategic marketer. He led his company, Kotler Marketing Group (KMG), to work for Fortune 500 multinational companies. In 1999, he was invited to open a branch business in China to provide strategic marketing consulting to Chinese state-owned and private companies, and in the development of high tech campus parks for medical devices and advanced manufacturing. KMG China employs 50 professional staff and has offices in Shenzhen and Beijing. Mr. Kotler is currently chairman of Kotler Marketing Group. His son, Tony Kotler, is President of Kotler Marketing Group USA. Cao Hu is President of Kotler Marketing Group China.

Milton Kotler is a violinist. He served both as an instrumentalist and chairman of the board of the Washington Symphony Orchestra from 1990 to 2000. He is an author of six books and lives with his family in Washington, D.C. He and his wife Greta have four children, Tony, Josh, Jonathon, and Becca, and four grandchildren, Jacob, Sarah, Caleb and Jack.

Final Impressions